ALSO BY FRANZ WRIGHT

Poetry

Wheeling Motel *(2009)*

Earlier Poems *(2007)*

God's Silence *(2006)*

Walking to Martha's Vineyard *(2003)*

The Beforelife *(2001)*

Ill Lit: Selected & New Poems *(1998)*

Rorschach Test *(1995)*

The Night World & the Word Night *(1993)*

Entry in an Unknown Hand *(1989)*

The One Whose Eyes Open When You Close Your Eyes *(1982)*

The Earth Without You *(1980)*

Translations

The Unknown Rilke: Expanded Edition *(1991)*
No Siege Is Absolute: Versions of René Char *(1984)*

The Unknown Rilke *(1983)*

The Life of Mary (poems by Rainer Maria Rilke) *(1981)*

Jarmila. Flies: 10 Prose Poems by Erica Pedretti *(1976)*

KINDERTOTENWALD

KINDERTOTENWALD

Prose Poems

FRANZ WRIGHT

Alfred A. Knopf
New York
2011

THIS IS A BORZOI BOOK
PUBLISHED BY ALFRED A. KNOPF

Copyright © 2011 by Franz Wright

www.aaknopf.com

Knopf, Borzoi Books, and the colophon are registered
trademarks of Random House, Inc.

Library of Congress Cataloging-in-Publication Data
Wright, Franz, [date]
Kindertotenwald : prose poems / by Franz Wright.—1st ed.
p. cm.
"This Is a Borzoi Book"
ISBN 978-0-307-27280-5
I. Title
PS3573.R5327K56 2011
811'.54—dc22   2011011554

Front of jacket: Painting by Michaël Borremans,
Sleeper, 2007–2008. Courtesy Zeno X Gallery, Antwerp.
Photo by Peter Cox
Jacket design by Carol Devine Carson

Manufactured in the United States of America
First Edition

This book is dedicated to my wife Elizabeth
and to our friend Deborah Garrison.

As for me, I have not been the unfortunate messenger of a thought stronger than I, nor its plaything, nor its victim, because that thought, if it has conquered me, has only conquered through me, and in the end has always been equal to me. I have loved it, and I have loved only it, and everything that happened I wanted to happen, and having had regard only for it, wherever it was or wherever I might have been, in absence, in unhappiness, in the inevitability of dead things, in the necessity of living things, in the fatigue of work, in the faces born of my curiosity, in my false words, in my deceitful vows, in silence and in the night, I gave it all my strength and it gave me all its strength, so that this strength is too great, it is incapable of being ruined by anything, and condemns us, perhaps, to immeasurable unhappiness, but if that is so, I take this unhappiness on myself and am immeasurably glad of it and to that thought I say, eternally, "Come," and eternally it is there.

—Maurice Blanchot,
as translated by Lydia Davis

*Strange parents, who so easily can be
Like friends to me, a twisted son like me.*

—H. Phelps Putnam

CONTENTS

KINDERTOTENWALD

WINTERSLEEP

I was having trouble sleeping. I don't know how long I'd been lying there and listening to the blizzard when I had the most vivid impression that it was a blizzard in Minneapolis in 1959. And I found this disturbing. I knew it would now have to turn on its lamp, get out of bed, and try to write about me; and of course no matter what it wrote, I would just sound like something it had made up. But in the end it decided to stay put, turn over, and keep me to itself. I think that was the right thing to do. After all, it was only a blizzard in Minneapolis in 1959. How are you supposed to describe something like me? And when you think about it, why should you try, why should you even care?

WOMAN FALLING

It's so interesting you should suddenly be here, how did that happen? In your favorite place, this witchy old orange orchard, the very spot where it gives the impression of stretching forever in every direction—all those spokes, from where you stand, between the trees, within sight of the three-story house painted the same shade of white and right about the same size as this lone beehive you stand looking down at a moment, no one has lived there for as long as you've known it, kept it a secret, parking off the highway and walking a mile down the nameless dirt road in a windy and shadowy brightness, wind from the sun you would say, in your mind, if I know you, as I do not, and never will now, no one will anymore, you have made sure of that, but I can picture you saying it, I'm not bothering anyone, I don't even know where it is, that's the point, no one did, nobody knew how to reach you, in the one vacant room with a mattress you even spent a night sometimes, honeysuckle southern California dawn wind blowing through the glassless windows and over your body, over your hair, maybe God would let you be the wind, but I don't know what God thinks either, I just like to imagine you all at once finding yourself in that place, walking along, without anyone knowing, that was the haunting, that was always the fun, and stretching before you a whole day of wandering and singing alone in the instant right before the one in which your body meets the earth at last.

NIETZSCHE'S MIRROR

The final breakdown coincides, it's said, with his botched intervention in the savage beating of a horse, the sight of which perhaps brought to mind the pedagogical methods employed long ago by Dad, the good pastor. The final train journey home is uneventful, safe arrival ensured by the company of burly individuals who, while not given to deep speculation, observe with increasing fascination the professor's inability to resist removing a small mirror from the inside pocket of his jacket every few minutes and studying minutely, with an expression of horrified astonishment, his own face. When questioned at last regarding this activity, or imagining he has thus been questioned, he replies, or so it seems, with a query of his own, succinctly posed: Is it true that I am here? After prolonged consideration involving, incidentally, the prefiguration and dismissal of Husserl's suspension of belief strategy, he continues without ever once moving his lips along this same track. If, as so appears, I actually am still present, how long can this state of affairs be expected to last? Approximately how long, that is, must I go on enduring it? And why? At this point it's conceivable that, having nothing better to do, he will begin the mental composition of a series of letters to be set down and mailed in material form later, bearing the singular signature of "The Crucified One," and addressed to a variety of European dignitaries, suggesting in the strongest possible terms the military overthrow and occupation of his German homeland. In long retrospect, the reaction to these urgent messages is not difficult to imagine. So much the worse for the recipients. It will be a couple of decades before his mad admonishments may be perceived for what they were, a pretty damned good idea, if anyone recalls them at all; and how unfortunate for the millions of slaughtered young men who have not yet been born. Oh well. They will be mailed, nevertheless, after he has been delivered into the care of his mother, a fate I would prefer not to dwell on. During the eleven years that remain to him, confined to his old boyhood room, he will soon lapse into more or less total silence—I know I would—broken only on occasion by a lengthy and unpunctuated scream.

THE WALL

Be it ever so scarred and unstable, the table you write at belongs right in front of a mirror, so spoke the battered master, to my knowledge the single author that magnificent and winged lunatic Rimbaud ever deigned to admit admiration for, think of it. At this time the poet was fortunate to have the use of a table and mirror, not to mention a room where he could concentrate, as he occasionally managed to, in spite of the distractions involved in dealing with some of the semiliterate individuals who then as now were known to enter the literary profession as if for the sole purpose of hounding and tormenting anyone with the poor judgment to show some actual talent for writing. I have a preference for blank walls myself, though I certainly never would have said so in his presence—in his presence I very much doubt I would have been capable of articulating opinions or thoughts on any subject whatsoever. Windows are out, however. No windows. I have enough trouble with what I can see through the wall. Only a minute ago I was watching him pass by, and to judge by the look on his face, I am afraid he was going through one of his brief stretches of addresslessness, caught between the gentle hospitalities of one poetry-loving landlord and the next, the austere amenities of one unflushing toilet of an apartment and another; he was limping slightly, as though he had on two left shoes, finally stopping to rest on a vacant park bench, it wasn't raining that hard, vomiting tactfully first in some bushes nearby, probably nothing, a touch of opiate withdrawal, there'd been no indication of alcoholic seizure, and as it was relatively unlikely that food had been ingested in a while, he made no mess to speak of, a mere ounce or so of some sort of green liquid which blended in well with that damp and verdant scene. As he did not appear to be carrying a notebook, thankfully there would be no need to make use of his aching knees, which had so often served quite nicely as a desk that allowed him to hunch his thin shoulders and slowly bend forward to shield his page from the various forms of precipitation so prevalent in his part of the world. Evidently he'd misplaced his pen, as sometimes happens, so his left hand would not be required to take the place of stationery. He was spared, as well, the possibility of injuring himself as he had once, unfortunately, during a mild and near-unprecedented instance of self-mutilation, well, there had been no more than a few shallow puncture wounds, resulting from the understandable frustration that might accompany being reduced to recording on his own flesh one of the few lines of genuine poetry ever written. He remained on his bench for an immaculately inconspicuous and legal length of time, his somewhat deranged head all the roof he'd be enjoying for a while yet, his only mirror a shocking but swiftly curtailed couple seconds of eye contact with an elderly woman who happened to turn to him in passing her crumpled, thrown-away face. Putting up his collar, he slowly got to his feet, staggering in a manner that was practically unnoticeable, and doing a marvelous impression of somebody not crushed by dread as he moved on, soon lost from sight in the rain, which was not really falling that much harder.

THE POET
(1644–1694)

To suddenly perceive the world as if it were something you had never seen before, and to grasp for an instant, mutely enduring the shock of total comprehension, the outrageous unlikelihood of being here to witness it, and of its being there at all—this is a matter of grace, but also a cruel and conditional ecstasy, one no mental effort can prolong, one that in fact consists of the grievous poignancy with which it bleeds away, fading and vanishing almost before it has fully begun, lasting only long enough to leave you with the familiar sense of missing out on something, raised to a more desolate power by the discovery of what it is. *Look at this staggering sight—new leaves shining with a light that's come here from the sun.* Even if they can't recall it, or outright deny it, everyone knows of this eerie event for which they found no name. But how many will spend their days readying themselves for what may well never recur; how many will devote the rest of their lives to the preposterous discipline of waiting, waiting and maintaining constant vigilance for a glimpse of what they can no longer see; of inwardly orienting themselves to a direction that does not exist. And who among them will gradually shed, year by year, every vestige or hope of a place in the world, becoming increasingly familiar with the taste of fear? This is no occupation for an adult who can look other adults in the eye, carry his own weight, and count himself one of them. *I just don't understand how a grown man could spend his time doing something like writing poetry.* This was not a career, this was a fate, a disaster. *Hand in hand the blind child and his mother stand admiring the new cherry blossoms* forever because someone spent his life watching for them, and preparing to endure once again a condition of illumination, then exercising the mastery that enabled him to store it in its purest form for the benefit of others, most of whom were not yet born, before moving on, exhausted and ill, and by now without even the hope of returning to rest in the comfort of the little house his friends had made available, dear to him once and now, in his feverish delirium, comfortably surrounding and sheltering him once again like the bronze shell of the snail that has blindly strayed from the tall grass to cross a damp dirt road and intersect, as it was born to, with the great wheel getting closer. And if, in spite of having perished of old age at forty-nine over three centuries ago while making his way on foot across the fields and mountains of Japan, Matsuo Bashō were to appear in this country of millions of aging adolescents on the first day of class, in need of an advanced degree, having lost his or used it to make a small fire in another time, chances are only one of his classmates would ever have heard of him, the one who never raises her hand, I'll bet, stunned into smiling for the first time in history and hurriedly making a place for him next to her.

MANUSCRIPT SCORE OF MESSIAEN'S QUARTET FOR THE END OF TIME

By the rivers of Babylon . . .

Where is your hand now, architect of the unseeable, syrinxes' harpist and departed sower of this rainbow made up of the voices of extinct birds perched as shivering notes along barbed wire? Do you remember that place, still endure it, like a slight limp, or a small undivulgable homesickness, are such things erlaubt where you are? That place where no one would dare weep, let alone sit down. Where the captors required of nobody a song, indifferently allowing yours; even listening politely with their sad attack dogs' eyes awhile. Before shrugging, and getting back to work.

HISTORY

I own a black shirt that once belonged to Frank Stanford. Rather, it was given into my care: I had this honor. It was presented to me in San Francisco one morning in June of 1980, three months after my father's death in New York. Later that same day I went on a long walk in hopes of locating the Douglas Elementary School where I'd attended fourth grade in 1961. Finally I turned a corner and there it was. My school, however, the street on which it stood, and the neighborhood itself had grown so much smaller. It would have made more sense if they had gotten larger, so great was the deterioration in myself. As I climbed the last block I practically tripped over the body of an enormous ivory owl, its wings spread there on the sidewalk, perfectly intact, its eyes closed as though sleeping in flight. I should say, parenthetically, that I hold no one to blame if they refuse to believe this—I had a lot of trouble believing it myself. I was wearing Frank's shirt at the time. A poet should always be wearing some black, he once said, according to the friend who had given it to me. In return I plucked one feather for her. There are three worlds. We know them as the three words present, future, past. And from here it looks like I was standing for a minute, at the age of twenty-seven, in all three of them at once. Anyway, that I stood there is a fact beyond dispute, even if it is only briefly recorded somewhere in the infinite pages of the history of unnoticed events. The shirt has grown too small for me, it is like the shirt of a good child: I keep it in a special drawer, folded formally, like a flag, and have always done so in the many different places I have lived over the years. It helps me, taking it out. At this point my opinion is that a poet should carry death's imminence with him at all times, the way a priest might his black book of extremely small psalms.

to C

THE YES

Each day for years, it gets up at first light, lets the dove out and stands in the doorway looking at the soft blue Arkansas sky without waking. But never you mind, it will be packing its small suitcase soon; it will leave the keys dangling from the lock and set out at last. Across the raven's brook and barefoot through the pathless wood of books, already it is traveling toward me, somehow I know this. Though blinded as I leave the outer brilliance. Though the stench of urine hit me like a blow and once more, in the blink of an eye, I am back at my watch, pretty mauled by a vicious cycle, right in the middle of raising a twenty-pound shot glass toward the general vicinity of my lips the way a ruined jeweler might gradually guide, from long habit, the loupe to an empty eye socket. But the suicides you always have with you. Maybe I'm just cruising around late at night. And waiting at what is already the longest red light in the world, no other car in sight, never will be, not in my private city, scared, sick. I'm the very lost person, the VLP, abandoned to man by himself this glass-bottom space station: one more ragged meat bone we'll always have haunting us, floating in a gray soup of its own filth and misery, what are you going to do. Let's say later on I happen to hang a sharp left for no reason I can think of, at an unfamiliar corner, just in time to glimpse a small three-legged dog making his way down the black sidewalk, and finally I ask to be given a new name, which nobody knows, and a new heart. In ascending progressions, the first dawn waves traversing that universe where the more you disappear the more vividly present you become, where the slower the velocity the sooner the time of arrival, the answer is on its way.

1997

14

DEEP REVISION

I look up from this unfolded page I've discovered (for the hand has its memories) in my back pocket to find that you are gone. After some more time has passed, time spent decoding its runic and largely illegible messages meant, clearly, for these eyes alone, surprise!, a pen appears in my hand; and while I myself might appear to be nothing but somebody's body hunched down between low grassy dunes, shielding itself from the cold, I am already traveling back, I am elsewhere, alas, very elsewhere, amen. But when I look up, you're still gone. And does this put a stop to it, whatever it is I am doing, wherever I am? That the thoughtful thing, at this point, might be to interrupt my work, or whatever it is I imagine I've been doing all my life, and take a walk in search of you, occurs to me. It does. And do I follow through; does he so bestir himself, you may well ask. Not I. I am already off again, a new obstacle having presented itself in the form of numb fingers requiring a glove, then their somewhat hampered progress once sheathed in thick black leather padding, not to mention the mind's, now distracted by hand's new resemblance to that of some non–*Homo sapiens* primate's, a gorilla's, say, one struck by lightning and oddly thereafter compelled to take up composition, not of lyrical fragments, let's hope, for its sake, as surely it stands a vastly improved chance of making a living by authoring a mass-market novel, perhaps the ever-popular memoir—in its case, one bound for bestsellerdom, clearly. I look up, and still you are nowhere to be seen, still unfound. Leaving me bereft of any company but that of low-grade terror in the guise of the winter Atlantic, that windblown dark emerald and seemingly infinite plane upon whose horizon we one day so long ago, in our frail craft, first appeared, God forgive us, the battered catastronauts. Though to look on the bright side, so too did the disillusioned Jefferson, no doubt doubly depressed now, on his way back from France, illustrious runner-up for best failed and betrayed revolution—I can almost see his still faraway sail, wind suddenly tearing the page from my fingers, goodbye, goodbye lousy page, childless kite, white shirt left on shore by the swimmer who will not be needing it anymore. The overarching dilemma remains, increasingly remains, as the early dark deepens: no you. I am ready to confess, it's beginning to get to me; and by way of emphasis, I am fully prepared to stand up here before the first merciless stars, in silent beseeching, to look up and down, to look both ways, to call out if need be. Which way have you gone? This winter beach, this narrow desert, it isn't all that long. What is wrong with me? How could I have lost track of you? I know that it was just a little walk you went on, tactfully allowing me to concentrate. And I am concentrating all right, my mind filled, to the exclusion of all else, by a small evil voice *oh see her walk, whitely walking on the waves.* And this is all bullshit, I don't even want to work, I am sick to death of it. I don't want to write anything, ever. I just want you.

AS WAS

You may be the beast right now but one day, rest assured, of something you are going to be the gory feast. Take me. The arrow found me in the end, one I myself had so long ago blindly let fly, what the hell was I thinking? Eyebrows may well be raised, I know mine are, at the attribution to my younger self of a capacity for thinking in any form; however, that the party was over—the party, the war, or whatever it was we'd been playing with—even I could grasp. Over and done with. You looked around and it was just a fact, incontrovertible if somewhat eerie, a kind of out-of-house experience or fallout shelter without walls. And in rage and confusion I took aim at the sky. Then I forgot all about it, immediately relapsing, and taking up again the scarlet thread of my interminable reverie. At this point I think you might want to sit down, pour yourselves a drink, and fasten your seat belts in preparation for what I am about to divulge. It is conceivable, some might go so far as to say highly probable, women are already a prominent feature of that impregnable daydream there at my desk, which has grown, I am sorry to say, a bit small for me, kindergarten of the damned I keep having to repeat. But I stray. And let's not forget it was I who was there, sole witness to that lost but indelible dawn on which they were destined to appear, each in her own small white ship. Sporting identical murderous glances, and displaying between bared breasts the identical tattoo, a lidless eye surrounded by a crown of thorns, wave after wave of them wading ashore in barefoot destitution and commanding me to kneel, I can still see it!

It's them, every last woman I have ever slept with—can beheading be far behind? To be fair, it's still possible I am absorbed in something entirely different, an image, say, or an immense country I happened to be traveling through during what turned out to be my final moments (and aren't they all), right before the erect feathered shaft came flying and finally struck me from behind, and serves me right.

FORECAST

We are the monsters and beget monsters. Litter of mouths, look at that. We are the monsters, each in our own special way, with our own unique form of amnesia, nest of gaping mouths, born blind, our faces bathed in God's shadow, the sunlight. Each of us born with the right to ignore, until they die of neglect, the powers of forgiveness and foresight. We are the murderers, murderers murdered by murderers. Light on its crutches has no comment. We are the heirs of the murdered, it looks like we're born with a taste for revenge, a readiness to take our turn at becoming one of the murderers, then one of the murdered again. The Word in its wheelchair maintains its unbridgeable silence. Reserving judgment. For our startling alacrity when it comes to casting the first stone is matched only by our eagerness, an instantaneous willingness to risk our own lives to save a stranger's, oh blind light, its eyes filled with tears. I know I'm not supposed to say these things. Too late; I already said them. Then I drew the queen of sleep, if I remember right. Is this the ocean or the desert floor? I drew the ace of heroine to soothe my tortured animal. It's now a major felony for me to be alive, and they can have it. Over the forest rose a red moon, presaging autumn, the honey of death, great healer, infallible cure-all. I was drawn to the edge of the world, those nameless counties where the hexagon is hammered out in all its inexhaustible forms, from snowflake to witch-beckoning signs identically scarred in owl-crucified hulls, struts and ribs of wrecked north country barns, to the cells of disappeared bees who are the divinities and will not, by the way, go on indefinitely believing in our existence; whose own vanishing, when it is complete, will spell our own, so let's get a move on. Kill everything, everything. In a minute. First give me a chance to get over the shock of my sudden and bloody arrival here: evacuated, cast out from the infinite with which I had been one substance forever. And okay, those others were there waiting to greet me, happy to see me, what acting, eager to take me home with them, clothe and feed me, in love and awe enthrone me, &c. But I will get over it, one way or another I am going to find my way back and let the good times roll. When you get to the fork in the road, it's not an audition, and it's not an interview for a job. There will be no angel armed with a great sword of fire. But what are you supposed to do, just stand there with a bewildered and obsequious look on your face? I'll probably go the way everyone else does without even thinking about it. Sooner or later, like most everyone, I will get down on my hands and knees baa-ing obligingly, offer my throat to the knife, and move on. But you never know. There is still an outside chance that I will choose correctly, I may have done so already, so long ago, unknowing and unknown—all I can say is my hand is still shaking, the better to tumble the dice, I suppose. Deep down I am on the right track, I can feel it, I can see it. And if I misplace the dice, I'll remove both my eyeballs, spin around a few times, like the lock on a safe, like the hands of a clock, like the six-chambered cylinder of the old revolver used once before and only once in the familiar death-daring pastime. I'll spin until I stop, until I get a firm shove from behind and am off. I won't be able to see where I'm headed, but I'm not getting on my hands and knees, I don't care what they do. They're not going to do shit. I'm on the road again, white blindness; I'll be there, road unfolding like an endless bandage, road of it is not so much a matter of arriving as it is of never turning back. Then it will be time to sing.

ONE HUNDRED AND FIRST REASON
TO STAY IN YOUR ROOM

I was just coming from a visit to my doctor. Not the medical one this time, though they both work for the same company. One of those inimitably dark April days in Boston, the cold returned, though not in a big way: gray, drizzly, brain still closed for repairs. It was then I noticed the squirrel crossing the deserted Common. This was over in the northwest corner, where they used to deal with the witches and Quakers, those dangerous conspirators; and on desolately chilly days like this, the warmth from the fire alone would have drawn quite a crowd. I'm making that up. We didn't burn them anymore, like those European barbarians; we just hanged them, in the cold, within sight of the governor's office but far enough away to keep from disrupting business there in the great gold-domed statehouse on the hill. I've had a couple occasions to wander its oddly dim myopia-inducing hallways, and the only thing I remember with any clarity is the big round stained-glass window depicting a Native American shaking hands with the pilgrim in his preposterous uniform, the one who has braved exile and the terrifying sea to worship as he saw fit and make sure you do too. It had crossed my path from left to right, frozen in midflight, and looked me in the eye, shivering. I had never seen a squirrel shiver. For a minute it made me feel like I was dying. Thank you for coming to help us, the naked Caucasian cartoon of an Indian is saying, forever, in an arc of English words across the sky.

ABANDONED LIBRARY

Hive of the single unknown astronomically large but precise number of words that begin reappearing the moment I enter, slowly developing on their closed pages. And check this out, clearly we've reverted to the honor system, nobody manning the desks, and in all of this gigantic building not a single staff member to be found. No readers either. Has it been that long? And if no one has the desire to peruse these words ever again, it is so strange—where did they all go? Even those grim recluse cobwebby beings you could always count on, gone. And one can't help but wonder, what is he up to these days, grave little bookworm with the odd name? Not particularly welcome at home, or anywhere else for that matter, mind reader of the great dead by default, come out, come out. Always alone, to this very day, star-told? That's correct. Sorry. But I have come back, faithful to all of you—I'm not the same one, almost though. I have read more. A lot more. I am taller. I'm ugly. I'm tired. And if nobody sees me, I am not here, am I. And if no one is near, I'm unknown, I'm alone, a mere bone of myself, my own ghost. And I am walking again, very slowly, as though underwater, and taking much care, as when assigned to help the blind kid find his classroom. Evidently we are still searching, poor body, just look what's become of you. Wandering forever up and down the rows of dusty volumes, glancing left and right, a certain title escaping us, one which we seek as if it were the yellow-lit window we long to see, that place where we are not expected, a light snow beginning, not now, and not ever.

In the yard it is just getting light, as they say, and I wish I could meet them sometime and shake hands. I have been waiting all night for this, here by the one window, enthroned in his absence. I think it's a shame the way he missed out on the harvest, not to mention the first mist of leaves that northern April so far off now, the eighties they call it, the new president, the savior of greed, belly dancing demurely, looking everyone right in the eye and lip-synching over and over to his own cozy voice the money is green and getting greener. Starring in his own commercial, he came on every channel at once to say, Thanks for your vote. Now die and come back as a millionaire, have you no shame? Those crepuscular frogs are fading finally—where the hell is that sound coming from, anyway? It sounds like a distant symphony orchestra of Jew's harps perpetually tuning up. In the yard you can just about make out the ax they used; lodged in the old bloody stump, the handle seems to have bloomed overnight, the headless poor running rings around it. Maybe it's just me, but shouldn't they be in the barn laying our eggs at this hour? And where is that barn? Already sailed, I guess. Can't we get anywhere on time? Are you sure you are taking a multivitamin? You were only thirteen then, but it was the start of total war, guaranteed to last only three weeks or so—where was the general when you needed him? Probably still in his tent getting drunk on that case of absinthe Lincoln delivered to him personally on his darkest day, the better to sit still for his picture on the fifty-dollar bill. Exposure has taken longer than expected, as has mopping up of the insurgency, those penniless fools, will they ever give up? His skeleton is still sitting there in its canvas folding chair in front of the men in black hoods who are filming this movie out back somewhere. Your makeup's fine, what about mine? By the way, I'm pretty concerned about the way you sit at your keyboard all day staring into the sky-colored screen, looking up all at once when I enter the room as if someone has entered the room, overshadowed, I think it's called, between one instant and the next, very wet, in that place between the knees, between breathing and deathing, one pulsebeat, one wingbeat, one word (starry canyon between) and the next, one digital click of the night clock unheard, numerals never before seen dimming as, yes, it gets lighter out—doesn't it ever take a day off? Not a cloud in the sky, it says in this morning's paper, also saboteurs have used an itsy-bitsy nuclear device to destroy the mountain with the face of Crazy Horse gigantically carved in it, thereby unwittingly fulfilling his dying wish, and the work of replacing it with Barry Goldwater's has already begun. Who's she, you ask? Best not. I didn't hear a thing, did you? Probably drowned out by what sounds like the voice of a resurrected songbird, species unknown, who lives in yon tree (some say he is blind and cannot see), reciting the same black psalm over and over. And that's strange, seeing as how there are no trees here on this infinite plain blazing softly saffron in the morning star, can you see it? Don't look at my finger, look where it's pointing. That one right there, much smaller than the rest, just over those violet mountains. It's scaring the shit out of me, though not half as much as these walls which keep contracting to the size of the closet where bad children go, then moving away until they too—the roof having long flown away—disappear into the blue distance. You'd better get in here, that star's almost gone, and it's the only ceiling we'll ever have. It is the only fire I have to warm your hands.

When I am done puking I get up from the floor, wash my face, and slowly resuming an erect stance automatically look in the mirror. Whoa. In the first place, it isn't a mirror anymore but a window, and on the other side of this window, about ready to poke its head in, stands an enormous white horse, very gaunt, its gaze electric blue, the color of desert sky shining through the eye sockets of a skull. Now we're apparently going to get a sort of Mickey Mouse with bloody teeth. So things do not appear to be headed in an especially auspicious direction, and it is with some discouragement that I exit the bathroom and walk down the hall toward the living room where, after a journey of several years, I switch on the TV with the idea of checking out the action on CNN. It's not long before I discover that it is possible to weep from sheer astonishment and rage, I never knew that. The stained glass–gold light of the end of September falls through the window, creating the impression of a staircase, a steep and absurdly inviting one. All at once I am vividly aware of what this room is going to look like when I am no longer alive.

HOME FOR CHRISTMAS

Fifteen years later the old tollbooth keeper is still at his post but cannot break a twenty, regrettably, his brains blown out, or provide the forgotten directions. I did phone, what do you think? Before I can blink I am parked out front of the unbelievably small, unlighted house. I've got my finger on the buried bell, nothing. For hours I've been walking around, and I hate to be the one to tell you this, but no one is home in Zanesville, Ohio. My dusty toothbrush waits for me, of this I feel quite sure, my teenage image in the dust-dimmed mirror waits. Only now I'm afraid I'll be forced to disturb the slow fine snow of dust that's been coming down, year after year, on my blanket and hair, and put on my dust-covered clothes, and walk without making a sound, trailing my eternal lunar footprints, down the windless hall, and down the stairs at last. It's not going to happen overnight. But one of these days I'll arrive; I will go down to sit with the father. The elderly father, strictly speaking, of never really having been there. I will sit down and eat my bowl of dust like all the rest.

AFTERFLIGHT

A boring uneventful flight, the kind you pray for, and look, you can already see the sparsely lighted outer outskirts of your destination. But not so fast. It seems you will not be deplaning, if ever, without some fear, it's on the house. Indeed, we're finally going to have one of those yearlike fifteen minutes of that dread euphemism turbulence, thoughtfully forewarned first by the deep relaxed and soothingly authoratative male voice that seems to be coming from nowhere and everywhere, the one almost sleepily suggesting that you fasten your seat belt for a while. The tone is all. This time the pilot sounds like he has just ingested a 10mg Valium and downed a half pint of bourbon before having this brief chat at you, and that is a terrible, terrible sign. Instantly you're a profoundly frightened six-year-old being assured by your father that, no, forget about it, no way that tornado in progress outside, in the apocalyptic green light, is touching your house; the house next door, maybe, and that would be sad, but not yours; the father says, and therefore it shall surely come to pass. And so it happens! The plane straightens out, as it always has, slows to a glide, and is soon touching down in a fantastically convincing illustration of the advisability of survival over perishing in flames, surrounded by the screams drowning out your own, in an arctic fog at the height of what passes for rush hour in Anchorage, Archangel, or wherever the hell you are, and who cares where you are! How good it is to be alive! How grateful you are for your legs. If you could just get them to work, you might get yourself out of this machine and never come anywhere near one again. In the small airport bar I have been gradually printing the previous sentences, letter by letter, moving my lips, like somebody learning how to write again, stopping to cross out, revise, pause and stare into space, and generally attempting reentry into the sense of security and well-being typically enjoyed by the humble earthbound. Reentry into a normal sense of time. It's called the present. They had to call it something. And here it is, all around me, if I'm not mistaken. I think the fellow seated on the stool beside mine might be willing to provide corroborative reassurance; I don't imagine he'd want to argue about it. And I intend to inquire, I do, I think. But later. After all, it will still be the present. I am going to assume that at that hypothetical point in the future, it is going to be the present again. I find this extremely bewildering, and am doing my best not to think about it. I will clear my throat in a meaning way, turn to him, get his attention somehow, a wave of the hand, some conventional verbal salutation, shoulder, but later. I wonder what happened to the others, all the countless other presents. As for this one, just look at it, what a mess, so-so threadbare, I would like to say spectral, but I think that would be going a bit far, though you can almost see right through it in places. The present, instant by instant deleted, draining away, before it has even finished occurring. I am afraid, seriously afraid. Take everything, you can have it all back, but leave for a little the words, of all you gave the most mysteriously lasting; though deadly too, at every turn wrecking my life, in one way or another, as they gave me another, the life of someone I don't even know, and don't particularly like either. What else do you have planned? Just let me finish, though it hardly matters, the thing I so long ago promised to do. Don't take from me what took so long, not when it is almost finished, that would be fairly cruel, if you ask me. You to whom all time belongs, can you see that little boy, absent from class again, walking the tracks by himself, aimlessly wandering the alleys of Minneapolis, kicking through dead leaves, then all at once the streets of San Francisco in the late-afternoon fog soundlessly cresting Twin Peaks in slow motion in 1963. I spent the summer walking all over that city, I lay awake at night waiting for a hydrogen bomb to fall on my house. And wandering alone once, I felt something touch me, I stopped dead, I watched as time stopped, possessed by affection and kindness toward anything, anyone, so the hunter himself is scented, the emboldened prey circling back around and soundlessly approaching from behind, taking its time, all the fleet weapons of death useless now, quiver empty, no rounds, and changed in his grasp back to a stick or a stone.

I AM IN A CHAMBER OF LASCAUX

Day after day a man long dust is dying back into the work again, under the ground, where whether it is day or night is neither known nor especially relevant to anyone. By torchlight or torch-dark, a little more blind with every return to the world tens of thousands of years before Plato, he rapidly continues on. With nothing but his scarred nameless hand and a mind repeatedly struck by lightning-brief instants illuminating things that no one else can see, things he knows he will never remember among one or two he must instantly memorize. With nothing but the brush he himself made from the hair of the one he is trying to call forth, to coax into this world below, into living forever, show that something can. For whose eyes? Now the brush seems to move on its own, lightly tugged at like a fishing pole or water-seeking stick guiding the hand that disappears little by little as what it is doing begins to become recognizable. A man vanishes into the rock of ceiling or wall as he draws from it beings who were not there before, in the Sistinelike darkness, the brush become a wand with which he is summoning from the Creation one of its creatures, suggesting the presence of the whole ravenous manivore universe overhead; then masterfully, calmly painting beyond into the creature in glory and, by doing so, opening a dilating crack to another, a universe in glory. This creature is no image, no reflection in a windless pool of water, but a being that weirdly surpasses the model, suggesting a place beyond this stench of souls, the coughing and muttering of those soon to enter the earth and never return. This animal is like words, which can mean what they say and something cunningly different as well. Black flying clouds of bison, rainbow horses, great deer flowing endlessly . . . In his new universe populated by animals exceeding in beauty even the imperious divinities of the first sunlit world thundering overhead, beings possessing the powers to endure and dominate that terrifying place, a stick figure only he renders himself. Why is he there at all? No one's ever been able to recall where they came from, or where the road that brought them here is hidden; no one remembers what they were seeking, the first to set out walking, what higher home, beings like him, the stick figure glancing at the stick of brush in his left hand. Some have tried to rest the hearts that drove them this far, tormented by a sense of the home abandoned long ago or the one not yet found; torn, they stay, their wanderings ended. Others have moved on, in time all will have to, driven south by the cold, these chambers and labyrinths left vacant, all memory of them either torn to pieces abruptly and eaten, or gradually forgotten. At some sites he seems to have left his blank handprint behind. Not in signature, not to say who he was. To a man like this, who he is might best be described by a snowfield showing no evidence that anyone has crossed it. It is relatively certain he has never spent a second of his life wondering what others not yet born might say about him or what he has done. He is the passing on of the methods as they were passed on to him, by his father, his mother, or one of many others who don't live with him anymore, visibly. He is infinite humility, he is happiness, the nameless genius hiding away, for the eyes of the unseen alone, high up in the shadows of Chartres' northern wall his *God While Creating the Birds Sees Adam in His Thoughts.*

BLADE

If I stare into it long enough, the point comes when I don't know
what it's called, a condition in which lacerations are liable to occur,
like a slip of the tongue; when a single drop of blood might billow
in a glass of water, blooming in velvet detonation and imparting to
it the colorless, tasteless, and sourceless fear in which I wake.

1975–2010

MORNING MOON

She is only a local TV morning news anchor vaguely suspected of leading a second life as a soft porn star, and this is so unfair. The poor thing can barely walk nude past a full-length mirror without blushing. Perky, a perpetual jogger, and the very trellis of fashion—she prides herself on remaining at all times at least fifteen seconds ahead of it. Lately she has been subsisting on portions that would leave a spider famished, is that how you say it here? Every last hair in its place, poised and beaming; milk-white mask and gash of lipstick applied with immaculate care at all times, even now, napping bolt upright in bed, one small breast exposed, pale as a wax-apple blossom in its coffin, far from home, thirty minutes at least, and sadly missed.

But in truth, as everyone knows, the moon is a fairly elderly party. Very often it stays up all night, and can even be glimpsed in the dawn sometimes, looking a bit like the single lit window of some solitary author's high apartment.

The moon's a dead rock, but I still like the word, so black in its white space.

Sometimes it's not there at all. But it's there. Gaze of the unseeable, and the long lampless waters; vertical stare at the tug pilot on the East River drinking his coffee, or the guy doing lines of cocaine in the snowplow through the night hours.

Fellow night workers, what can we say to the moon except *You again?*

You again.

Little Miss Death's Head, ghastly prop; face of a child pretending to sleep in a far country.

TRANSFUSION

Strange, I suffered from none of these symptoms until I was so intensively treated for them. Now I'm always freezing, and have evidently been shattered into five or six chattering replications of myself, all leaning in utter exhaustion on very thin canes made of glass.

I remember the night we were torn like a page from our sleep:

I, your telephone, command you to report to the ER without delay.

The last thing you see is the first.

This time it seems I woke up with pneumonia, anemia, tuberculosis (further tests will be required), crucifixion by toothache, a shadow by night, &c. Clearly, I will never be the same. Yet you are with me.

To your entire satisfaction has anyone described the look of love? Mine neither; but I have seen it.

I'm seeing it right now.

I am traveling up the beams of your eyes. I am slowly being lowered into a place of light.

Now, this picture that has come into my keeping, it must be thirty years old. The fall of Vermont. The Vermont of the past, one of them, in mist, remote mountain one red blaze of maple. Three friends walking a back road, the one invisible, the other turned toward the camera in the grip of hilarity, as if to say *Just look at this guy.* Meaning me. I am turned in his direction with eyes directed at the sky above his head and smiling benignly, perhaps somewhat sadly, but smiling: I have the impression that my soul, knowing better than to bother, is gazing at things unseen, as well as the far-off boots supporting it. The body seems happy enough, hands shoved into pockets, shoulders thrown slightly back, triumphantly young and to a ninety-nine percent probability, triumphantly high at that moment, so what? In spite of various stumbling blocks, such as near-homeless and penniless unemployment at the age of twenty-six or so, it seems genuinely content in this particular instant of its pure nothingness, displaying a peaceful disdain for the necessity of anything whatsoever except the love of his friends and the present. Pretty good-looking guy, one who looks like he's all packed. I don't know what happened to that face, some sort of ineluctably long-acting acid or something. And look at me, with my vestigial vanity, still the same idiot who believes not that he is indestructible and can do without a job or a home, but that if he could only get home, if he could go home to stay (traveling incognito as the busted-up and fucked-over old guy he actually is), age would leave his body and he would be young again. There's only one problem. Which home would we be referring to? Because I can feel it, it would take more years than I have to go back, to find them all, and stay awhile, and see.

THE CHILD PSYCHIATRIST

The child psychiatrist will not be seeing any patients this evening. Not until she has cleaned up her vegetables and finished her homework, and that's all there is to it. Afterward she is perfectly free to meet with you alone, even to sit on your knee like a cheerful ventriloquist's dummy; or should she so choose, lie down on the couch and ask that you tell a story, your most beautiful and sinister story.

for Janet Wozniak

THE WOUND

The grave wound that receives prompt attention nearly always does well over time; where protocol is strictly adhered to, even your more hysterical lacerations stabilize readily, and respond rapidly as a rule to appropriate meds, toward which they display minimal resistance, gradually resuming a productive, socially active, and generally well-adjusted life. Interestingly, a number of more or less identical traumas never seek treatment at all and yet, once again with the passage of time, appear to enjoy a total recovery. And for reasons not presently understood, a certain percentage of much less deplorable injuries fail to respond to the most radical efforts: flatly refusing to cooperate, these minor gashes may remain a source of endless concern, irritation, not to mention financial anxiety both to their families and to society at large for years if not decades to come. They are certainly going to require close monitoring—they'll need to be examined, probed, and prodded, their condition reevaluated on a regular basis. And any lasting improvement is far from assured; on the contrary, I'm afraid. Too often we have stood helplessly by and watched as they regressed before our eyes into obsequious and attention-seeking whiners and—I can find no other way to express it—obsessively manipulative, widely read, and bizarrely prescient authorities on their own deterioration. In an unprecedented instance, one actually requested permission to recite an original ode to itself! I can't say which was worse, the pity or the disgust. Thank God our fifty minutes were up. I rebandaged as rapidly as possible, all the while making it vividly clear, believe me, that no such behavior would be tolerated again.

for Denis Johnson

38

SOME RECENT CRITICISM

I'd been lying in bed reading forever in my starry yoke. I kept coming across references to my death, but I felt fine. Better than ever. It was fairly ironic, if you consider that it is I who initiated the petitions to have myself captured and put down without delay, an unfortunate but necessary measure in light of a clear threat to public safety. Do you know not a single individual was willing to sign, not even in my own neighborhood, having completely lost touch, apparently, with even the memory of having been loved.

I DON'T KNOW HOW TO TELL YOU THIS

It is so strange, one minute I'm in the city and the next I am on the dirt road in Maine, walking in the early summer woods beside a little girl I love and gazing off in the direction of some music I remember hearing years ago at this very spot, a phrase of spare piano music played very slowly, over and over again, coming from a place in the dense trees where no house is, and when I turn to look at her once more, she has become a beautiful young woman, a disturbingly beautiful young woman, if still somewhat short. And I am old. I look at my hand and it is an old man's—how will I explain this to people? But then the problem may never even arise. I stop a minute, look around: who says I will be coming back? I watch her going on ahead. Does she seem bewildered, tongue-tied? Nothing of the kind. Has her face become preoccupied, troubled, the light around her disappeared? Not in the least. Does she skip, twirl, or laugh no more? On the contrary. Is she halt with self-consciousness; has embarrassment or sadness overshadowed her? Not yet. It is as if she were six again and has just received a new dress she adores and so delights in that she's secretly vowed (within earshot of every-one) never to take it off again, not under any circumstances, wak-ing or sleeping, never ever! Now she is telling me about a dream she had. She says she met a girl who was her, except this girl was so thin, she appeared to be starving. And had the greenest hair. Then it occurred to her to ask the girl if she was dreaming now. "No," the girl answered, before she could speak. "Actually, I think you're awake."

KORE

How much you have longed for these crooked and overgrown paths overlooking a violent sky, a bright stormy sea. Kore, how much you have longed for: blind girl one step from the cliff's edge making your sure way, the wind your hair, your solitary smile dark crimson poppies no one's ever looked at. Which one are you, Kore? How can you tell for sure if you're allowed to be alive this month? Is there anything here that stands out, dear to you, something you can't bear to part with? Will you recall it, Kore, when you resume the throne above the leaden and motionless sea?

BEES OF ELEUSIS

Unless a grain of wheat goes into the ground and dies,
it remains nothing but a grain of wheat . . .

JOHN 12:24

The ingredients gathered, a few small red tufts of the dream spoor per sheaf of Demeter's blonde wheat, reaped in mourning, in silence, ground up with the pollen and mixed into white wine and honey. These stored forms of light taken under the ground. Taken by mouth. First those who by birth hold in secret the word; then placed on the tongues of the new ones, into whose ears it is meant to be whispered. Word murdered, forgotten so long ago, placed as a kiss on the lips of the soon to be no longer breathing who mean to enter death with open eyes, with mouths saying death, what death? We have no word for it in our country where the bride of a brighter oblivion reigns. Not the purple-haired god but the child queen, the raped girl, come back from the dead hand in hand with the child she conceived there, returned in a resurrected virginity, wind through green wheat. Present-day site of a minor refinery in Christ. Although by the tenth generation already the children of light ("in their dark garments") had trampled and smashed and generally raped the two thousand years of this precinct and its holy meal, intolerable mirror. Men who'd designed and bowed down to a law derived from the sayings of one who appeared here to say that the law is abolished, it is too late, all that is over with. Men who bungled their way through the next eighteen centuries before finally descending into the earth themselves, and what they found there they used, and we thank you for destroying the destroyers

42

of the world. And here at the end this is as good as any other entrance to the underplace, journey of the fallen leaf back to the branch, to the bees of Eleusis among olive blossoms, untroubled among crimson wildflowers. Four thousand years later: same flowers, same bees.

THE WINDOW

I know, it's all terribly mystical. So what. So is work; and work means something. It means that what you do, you do for someone else. You do it for someone who loves you, that's all, someone who misses and needs you, if you are so blessed. I had my work—mine caused a little trouble, but I did it. I did what I promised. End of sermon. Can I ask you a question? Those moths in November, where are they now, do you think? You remember. We'd see them each evening around three in the afternoon; first a few, a mere bucketful, and all at once millions, everywhere. The cold arrived, the cold that really means it, and they were gone. They simply vanished, the way we all do in the end, but what does that mean? What does it mean, to say "Where are they?" Where are we? We change, all right; but where else, strange fellow moths, is there to go but the world? I saw the first trillions of snowflakes today as the light was beginning to change, to darken, blowing and swirling across the bare fields and back roads. Like you and I, they did as they were told. To things already here, we were called forth and asked to join them, asked to live. Not forever, not even very long. But we are called forth, we are brought here, and we are not brought here to die. I've been looking at Edvard Munch's *The Sick Child,* for the first time since I was nineteen. The girl is sitting up in bed, a green blanket pulled up to her waist, the mother seated facelessly beside her to the left; her left hand and the child's are clasped, knitted together, like the spot where a broken bone has healed. Then there is the child's thinning hair, the poor skull showing through the sparse wisps of it: it makes you think of an infant's, the little continents of bone still closing. Hair the color of the red wine in the half-full glass that's glowing on a table in the

44

foreground, in the half-light. Her head is turned sharply to the left, her line of sight passing right over the woman's bowed head in the direction of some unseen source of light—I always thought it was a window, but who's to say it's not a mirror? I see that now. Face beaming or reflecting from the depths of resignation, with a small exhausted smile of utmost sweetness, an unmistakable expression of gladness toward the outer world, the sight of things exactly as they are, and expressing the sum of all knowledge regarding that world: it is still there. I gaze at her as in a mirror. This world was here before me, is now here, and will be when I am not. There is no sadness in my face, not my true face. My blanket is green, with here and there patches of brown showing through. So the grave has come into the bedroom. I am sitting up in my grave, I knew it. It comes right up to my waist; but it is not covering my face. It is still very far from covering my face.

OUR MOTHER

If we come from the ocean, first we came from the sky. Tell me, remind me. This sky is all the heaven I am able to imagine. Remind me, until I am changed: once here we remain always here, in your universe, breathing the breath the changed left us, my body already the leaves overhead and grass to be walked on, someplace hidden away, or maybe the surf, where someone not born yet will walk alone and undress; this flesh is your shadow, remind me. Let me feel you're near to bless me, one of the women come to the tomb early, while it is still dark, only to find that the stone has been moved from the space where the corpse had been laid, and that the space is empty, and you are standing at its entrance next to the other who is silently weeping. He has been waiting for her, crouching down and working in the earth as if he were the gardener; and without looking up at her face, he asks why she is crying. Only yesterday, she replies, the teacher's body was laid in this tomb; but the stone has been moved, and his body is not there. Sir, please tell me what they have done with it. Then he stood up and said, Mary? From the four corners of the world and this room, bellying curtain who stands nearby, where I am lying ill, never to leave, bride of the child. No need to leave the place of peace, faceless Mother in sorrow, printless feet, weightless touch; wings of the separate address book my friend kept, then, in the stranger time, the unending Greyhound trip, boyhood with no boy and early manhood with nothing but. It is all forever written down on a page in your keeping, the palm of my hand: outworld the world time, outheartless the heartless, so much meaningless fear, fear filling the sky, why, why this insane waste of time, the whole world one faithless Gethsemane—now destination, true north, and only home. Unforget me this day, but stay where you are. No need to come dressed in the colors of water, friend I meet everywhere, mother of starry blue space; and if the world cannot be saved, may each be saved in secret from the world. Don't waste a death on me; let me come to you.

BROTHERS

So I went out among the dead, a pint of whiskey in my head, and lay down between graves in the snow, and closing my eyes to the blowing snow looked into his eyes, the ruined teeth, the wincing smile. No one is lost in his own eyes: from our own unique viewpoint, we are never lost. And the lost too love their lives. They hate their lives and want to die, but they too are attached to themselves, know any number of good things regarding that entity nobody else could know, their gaze fixed on a past like no other, a place where there's a hope they still remember, still hold on to. We cannot see ourselves as lost, though anyone else can, and will jump at the chance to point it out. We do not see ourselves at all, mercifully. Know what it feels like when you are looked at with love or simple kindness? I look at him as if he were a stain. I can feel it eat away a place to live inside my heart that's getting larger all the time. For I am just like him but luckier. Luckier to a degree I would call an atrocity. And if so much luckier, why do I not spend some time to understand and befriend him once more, as in childhood, for a few years? Barely awake, before you can even open your eyes, you know it has happened. You sit up in bed and spend the next couple of hours wondering how you are going to get from your bed to the bathroom, and that is just the beginning—you would really rather sleep. You start to like sleep more and more. I wish I could be clearer about the horror. But that very term instantly causes the others to glance at each other, suppress a knowing smile, and get away from us, as fast as they can. Before they do, though, this time I want one of them to tell me who was in charge of tracking my brother's swift progress sleepward and ever more winterward, footprints suddenly come to an end, like an unfinished sentence in the diary of an elderly teenager working the night shift alone, held up at gunpoint and abruptly deceased, halfway across a black snowfield. Right outside Reno, Nevada, at four in the morning our time. People don't just disappear. Look at me and understand me. People don't just disappear, do they? Not without leaving a stain. Oh yes, the others are going to want to get away from us, and they do. Every last one of them. And I am so sorry for you. One would imagine that knowing firsthand what you go through, I might be of more help. But I will abandon you too.

POSTCARD

How's snowy frozen nowhere? I'd join you if I could. I must have misplaced the key in your dim wood, the yellow wolfsbane, I'll bet: an excellent cardiac toxin for arrows, in case of a subtraction in the family, as was only to be expected.

THE LAST

Now we will leave behind poetry and paranoia and get real for a while. This is now me speaking. It really is. At least insofar as I comprehend that term, and keeping in mind that in my case a degree of relativity is bound to accompany it, a range of entities.

Where to begin. At times when this so-called me is by himself and he is mad; all right, when I am by myself and very very angry, I will suddenly hear said self snarling with a viciousness and conviction that astound me: "Jesus Christ was a son of a bitch!"

I honestly can't help it; it leaps right out of my mouth before I have a chance to reconsider, or at least to bite down on and kill it, mouth filling with blood. And I ask you. Why in the world to someone unabashedly in love with that Person would such a shockingly cheap and ugly string of words even occur, much less make use of his mouth to pronounce themselves? Leaving him with little choice but to contemplate them, those dull jewels of self-loathing . . . I try to imagine kindly and considerate people I know saying something like that, and feel coming over me, each time it happens, a cold blush of hatred and shame.

Well. If you'd like to know why, and even if you wouldn't, I will present my theory on the matter. Actually it can be summed up in the single word Dad.

It seems likely these words come so readily to me because they are the very ones (among others even more inventive) I spent my early childhood listening to the poor man mutter, scream, or utter in that tone of voice someone might assume when threatening to kill you and meaning it.

I have worked it out mathematically, rounding it off on the charitable side, and it seems that by the time I was seven (when he suddenly and inexplicably left home), I would have overheard that absurd imprecation employed approximately one thousand times. It made quite an impression.

As is widely known, my father had a way with words. And believe me, he said other things too; things you do not want me to put in your mind.

I love my father more than any other human being I have ever known.

Want to hear another one? Okay—same saintly lover of animals and other people's children.

He abruptly appeared once, emerging from his study with a belt in his hand, completely nude (this detail still mystifies me, but it does possess the rhetorical virtue of being impossible to make up), and in an unspeaking, cold, methodical, and nude rage he beat the black puppy he had just the other day given me for happily running in circles and barking while he was attempting to type. I was four. Perhaps my sole vivid memory of being four is looking on while he whipped it; and he whipped it until it vomited.

The only person I have ever known who makes credible Miguel de Unamuno's mysterious admonishment to live in a manner that would render your early death a disaster to the world is my father.

One Saturday morning when I was somewhat older and my brother was just a toddler, he happened to be stumbling hysterically after that father, no doubt obliviously absorbed in grave matters of intellect or art; while I'm afraid my brother had other things in mind, clearly requesting in his way some little moment of comfort, affection, or simple attention only to find one of his forefingers severed by a bathroom door slammed in his face. But it's all right, they sewed it back on somewhere, and my brother doesn't remember a thing. I can recall waiting alone—an activity at which I was already highly practiced—for my mother and brother to return in the car. My father never learned to drive, you see; and besides, he was extremely busy in his study all during the time they were gone,

this being I was seeking all my life with despair, finding him here and there for a time, so I thought, and pressing on. The being I sought, always failing, always rising and trying again, all my life to become.

So it has always been, and so it always will be—no, not always, not before I was, and for sure not soon. And so I go on working, my peace, sundial of my death. I go on working, for the night is coming when no one may work. When no one has to anymore.

WORK

So I did it. In the end, I always have. Without hesitation, risking all in one throw of the dice I myself fixed to fail. When or where I can't tell, can't recall. The study of lost hours, maybe; the movable cell, the workshop abandonable in ten minutes, like the counterfeitor's or bomb maker's; maybe the street's roomless room, empty park, or one of approximately fifty rented rooms, how should I know. Always so much to keep track of, so much that could be done only when I'd failed, when I wasn't there, you should have seen it. I was nothing but an underlining finger in the texts of light, the vapor trail at dawn, green Venus like a pearl of uranium resting in an unclenched palm. By myself I am not a bad person. But it was always something, a language to unlearn, all that music to unhear. I had nothing to live on, mainly this ecstasy of love, of all that must be done in unrecorded solitude, like prayer or crime, and the fire that no one else can feel or see surrounds me still, setting me apart, I could have done that myself but no. I only have one hand, you know. To do what gave me light, that let me live and was a life of sorts, I forced myself at gunpoint to sign my name in duplicate, page after page without end, agreeing not to have a life, and that was it: in terms of tools or weapons, that hand was all I was given to work with, actually there were two of them. But I think one must have been a reflection, the right one, the dumb one, trembling as I forged my own signature. But never mind all that, you go on ahead, don't give up our place in this death march of dreamers, this landless nation of the alone who never got to meet. When they stopped for sleep, it was I who kept watch, still do. (Somebody has to, it is said.) I'll live when I'm dead. And like all past and future leaves, same ones alive, unborn or deceased, the pages said or still unsaid, this one too must soon be done. No I. And it alone remain.

IMAGO

From my cell I was staring at a cloud, a dog decaying in the woods, etc., as I took up the long-awaited sequel to my *Confessions*. By this time my hand was so far away that it looked like a small hairless spider whose progress I could hardly help but follow, from the corner of one eye, as it went on filling page after page in a note-book with words too small for anyone to read. I looked up and noticed my bars had turned to gold. And before I forget, I'd like to be the first to congratulate everyone who has not committed suicide up until now. Camouflaged and candleless congregation, the world will never know your names, never know of its debt to you, or what you suffered; with what uncomplaining anguish you sacrificed the one thing all hold most dear, most have in common, the sense of being completely different from anybody else—it just vanished at some point, having attained its sexually mature and winged stage. You had a great vision about it but told no one. We have misnamed death life and life death. You saw another world, and it was precisely the same as this one. This time you told every-one, until someone asked you very nicely to quiet down. And the weather—everything you have heard on that subject is a serious understatement. The scarlet horrors were preparing to file in for my ignominious obsequies, already they swarmed freely over my body. Then there was no weather. I can't tell you how perfect that was. As it happens, I had been gazing up at the dusk stars, as I can be found doing more or less day and night, for I like to think they are growing younger as I die, come by sometime and tell me what you think. Under torture—some atrocious form of tickling, for example—I guess I'd describe myself as a fairly good egg in hot water. Family motto roughly translates *April wizards bring May bliz-*

56

zards. We tend to be apprehended eventually, after a futile but all the more spirited attempt at first-degree self-impersonation; however, this is not the time for levity, we happen to be speaking of a serious medical good-night kiss. Traditionally we are then detained at a local mental facility known for its celebrated alumni, though in recent decades secret and permanent socialist elements in the government have seen to it that the lowest scum of humanity now appear to have open access to those once hallowed halls smeared with our shit and vomit. What I'm getting at is this: after a relatively brief stay, we are invariably released with some deranged doctor's or other's blessing, a mixture of relief and disgust on the part of the staff, and the secret eye-signal that will get you into any movie house in Milwaukee free for the next year. Some of us like to get together once a day, rain or shine, and gather furtively at the picnic grounds under those tall wavering candle flame pines, where neither moth nor rust can reach, nor faintest scream, and exchange ribald tales verging on satanic perversion, each drawing his iridescent injection from the same oceanic martini, very dry, about two tears' worth of vermouth, in an unremembered dream.

PORTRAIT OF TWO SAINTS

1. Saint Teresa of Ávila

When it had become clear that the deceased was not about to relinquish either the mysterious failure to rot or the pervasive and oddly annoying fragrance of roses in which she'd been lying in bed for some months wearing an expression of profoundly child-like happiness, shining eyes wide open, a white sheet pulled up to her chin, the final reaction of her associates was unpleasant, to say the least. It was as if such an unprecedented period of mourning, awe, enforced silence, and increasing bewilderment over how to proceed with the funeral had nourished and gradually allowed the dark gestation of a general but mutually unacknowledged wish until, in one sudden and uncontrollable venting of lust to acquire sacred relics, they simply tore the body apart. The ownership of its various limbs (and anatomically let's just leave it at that) was then savagely contested as if by black-cassocked gorillas. One hastens to add that this deplorable but surely unpremeditated behavior was instigated by a single individual acting alone, none other than Teresa's longtime acquaintance and confidant Father Gracián, who comported himself from the first in the most discreet manner, believing himself to be completely unobserved when he stole into the glowing silence of her room with the kitchen's meat cleaver concealed in his sleeve and a cutting board tucked deftly under his arm and, coughing loudly to cover the sound of the blow, hacked off one of her weightless white hands.

2. Bernadette

Sister Moth chewing and chewing through the night. Sisters Rust, Fungus, and Mildew, all three hard at work already, scrubbing each individual mirror and stone to a dull filthy green, a single tear of acid rolling down each of their cheeks. Meanwhile, Sister Maggot's busy kissing, one by one, the endless orphan infants in their cradles until she finds herself looming above the first one again, smiling in sudden recognition when it smiles at her. A sun begins to rise, revealing the hundreds of bodiless wheelchairs and crutches standing in a ring around the monastery walls, along with a lone white winged cane tap-tapping shyly at the back door. The locked door with the sign clearly stating that the child is ill today and will not be healing anyone.

CUTTING

All the Sylvia Plath fan clubs will be meeting on campus tonight, same as any other night, same as any other college, at undisclosed hours, alone in our dorm rooms busily calculating the number of carrot sticks we'll be allowed to consume the next day and occasionally scolding ourselves in funny voices, while we wait for it to be time to take powerful long-acting amphetamines, you know, our *meds,* the ones that help us concentrate better—definitely—on what we will soon be doing with our razors, oh see the great brightly lit party boat traveling faster and faster through the darkness toward a gigantic waterfall of blood.

When I get tired of staring at words on a page, owlet, when I am finally good and sick of marring white space with black ink, my hands and face filthy with it, cut off, immured in my own mind, then what? It is way past time to do something, but what? It is time to live, and look at me. At dawn I say good night, at night I say why did I wake, what kind of existence is that! Will I ever get some peace? Am I ever going to witness a form of beauty that is not the child of death? Remember the day long ago when you entered that place light never penetrates, place of so many hidden things you had no words for, and no one to talk to about them; how you wandered there so long you thought it would never end. Somehow you found your way through at last, leaving the child behind. Listen to me, destined to live in a world beyond ours, beyond anything I can imagine: the day is coming, though you will not know it, and will recognize it only gradually after it has long passed, when you will suffer no more. When all you needed will be yours. I think of Robert Desnos, among the other few liberated wraiths, shown to a quiet corner and given a cot to die; who remained alive as long as he did by incessantly composing the same poem to his wife; by holding her memory when he lay down in the night with his hunger and lice; by perpetually considering the reality of her life at every given moment. Who died before she could find him, though by that time he for all intents and purposes was her. If you love, he wrote, or wish to love, do not dream.

CAN YOU SAY THAT AGAIN

My stepfather was busy splitting my stepmother's skull with an ax, which struck me as excessive behavior even for him—oh, I see: she'd first flown in the window and, folding her black vespertilian wings, had bitten his neck pretty bad, which quite naturally resulted in instantaneous rabies, then their mutual demise, why didn't I think of that? A conical mountain rose in the distance, a road winding around and around it like the thread of a screw, on it children in white chadors descending slowly in song (the two of them reborn in their company), I never heard anything like it. Each then releasing from hands now unfolded from prayer scarlet moths who darkened the air, the sound of their voices like faraway choirs heard while dying by fire for the cause.

THE SCAR'S BIRTHDAY PARTY

Dim sun-checkered path through the forest, the perishing limbs loose their leaves; were they mine I would gladly let go all my gold leaves to carpet the ground her feet walk on, though she merely frown, forget I lived, and hurry on, for she must not be late; for reasons not at present time if ever known she can't be late. She hurries on. She knows only that they are waiting. They are waiting. They are longing for her at this very moment. All year long they have been pining for her, waiting and listening, listening through sleep for the steps they know, the little knock, the child she was they most intently listen for and wait. The child she never was but will be now, if somewhat tall, the instant the front door starts opening as though by itself and the option to enter is offered, apparently. They rejoice, at mere sound of her steps were already rejoicing, though no one will say so; no one knows how that is done, how to make the appropriate face, even. They wish in their way to delight at the sight of her, if it is the last thing they do, to grunt something in greeting, so great is their happiness that she has come, is standing there in person. But for her they have little to live for. It's dying they live for, in fact, and TV. Somebody hands the remote to her, this honor is done her, and gestures sit down. Want a Coke, want a cookie, they mutter, it sounds like that, eyes still intent on the set with the sound off, familiar room otherwise dark, curtains drawn. There in its light they all sit: Father Blind, Mother Monster, now her, the faculty of speech regressed already to that of a nine-year-old irreparably shy with terror, sick with hope. She can't say she is comfortable yet with being seated in this vast armchair, her feet barely touching the floor; or with the prospect of having to sleep in a bed half her length, in her old room, or lying there in utter darkness frozen, unable to move when they enter, tongue drawn back into her throat. But then she will be dreaming, won't she? The visit itself may be some kind of dream, that is still vaguely possible, a hope entertained, resorted to when necessary, when painful and unheard-of things were occurring to her body, for example, no cessation of them yet in sight, in previous years, those unending years of her actually living there, possessing no memory whatsoever of having woken up anywhere else. For the time being, she is still sitting here, right next to Mother the fixed smiling glare and her husband the mumbled joke nobody gets, they appear to be sleeping, reclined in their chairs, all year long they've been sleeping, sleeping as snow fell, blowing all around the house, spring branches tapping at windows, each alone in their rooms, summer fields white for harvest, then leaves, golden leaves falling, leaves of my dying, dying to see his eyes, hear his voice saying my name, once again he has come here to save me, to buy me things, teach me how monsters have monsters, that's right, the tormented torment, the abandoned abandon, charismatically numb, cold, surviving, the last ones left standing, and how shall they warm someone else so very much themselves in need of one to come and save them from that arctic horror they have been crossing on foot all their lives, the last companion eaten, the graves of my footprints erased long ago, dying of loneliness there in my cubicle, waiting for someone to rescue me, someone to rescue, it comes to the same thing. *Save me . . . I miss you . . .* All the while they were sleeping, they slept as the seasons were changing around them, waiting for this day, Mother Beat You Daily into Speechless Deafness, Father Blind to It All, *I'm sorry dear we just don't have the money for a hearing aid right now,* blue soundless TV, and look: there's Brother Rapist, unnoted, unmentioned, untraceable weeping ignored, ignored knock at the back door, the knocking that goes on and on, forwarding address unknown; and Sister Silent is sitting here too in the bad light, the perpetually downcast gaze, the amputated tongue, forever nodding yes yes yes as she's mouthing the words of the miniature Bible she carries at all times, never getting beyond the first page, from under her pillow it slowly recites itself, such a kind voice saying everything's fine, everything is going to be all right, abruptly followed by a stream of loudly whispered accusations, each one true! But he didn't really mean it, my peace, my beloved, while we're waiting for her to turn up, it seems like all we ever do, poor little elder sister still so far and maybe lost awhile but on the straight road once again, surely, and she shall wear gold, golden leaves to adorn her, to guide her here, nodding, now and then slapping herself in the face, hard, trying to shake off the dream she keeps falling into, earth opening under her, the dream of walking someplace else, anywhere, I must wake up now, she's saying, yes, she is so close, I can already hear her, but here in Kindertotenwald the way is long, the roads unnamed, etiquette strange, changing from day to day, minute to minute, for example: is it correct to comment admiringly on a family friend's shiny new fang dentures? There I can't help you. The house must be close by now. So what does one say this time, what does one do, when the sardonic greetings cease? You're asking me? Cringing hugs, possibly. Shake a chill and weightless hand. Kiss a cheek smelling faintly of stale lilac and rotting meat. Take an ax to them all, shrieking, exalted, hunting them from room to room, screaming the scream that will never be over? Beats me. And how did they manage it, do you imagine, all those years keeping their true lives concealed from the neighbors, and look at them now in their ultimate cunning somehow they have totally changed their appearance I mean past recognition you feel who are these shrunken frail elderly people who've taken the place of our parents and where did they bury them old people no one would ever suspect victims now think of that and abandoned nobody to care for them here in their long dusty nap with the grass growing up to the windows the household falling down around them all on account of this one thankless child Miss Big City fake blonde and self-centered daughter. Who cannot be bothered. Yet here she is again. And why? Why do we still go on phoning darkly fêted and fed by our torturers why did we not at eighteen leave and never look back and completely forget them, I know, the need from time to time the need to prove they're really there you can see them have proof that they actually lived are even living still at a listed address and not just in your head and besides. Where else did you ever fit in, tell the truth, and where else is a monster to turn, already so close, what else can you do turn around and go home, and what home would that be? Turn around and go back to that arduously perfected impersonation of one of the normal, fuck the normal, where were they when we needed them, and how could they know, how comprehend this poor sorrow, the guilt, the humiliating and undisobeyable hunger to somewhere belong, just to rest for a day, and be for once this crippled child and how much she has loved.

LAW

Either I was born without a moral compass or somebody took mine away from me and smashed it with a rock, presumably at one of the numerous schools I'd attended by the time I was twelve—institutions for the reform of semihuman prepubescent primates prematurely preoccupied with unpremeditated ejaculation, a noble goal, though one seldom achieved with anything like lasting success despite the best efforts of a devoted and discipline-oriented faculty, if one that suffered, for such was the age, from frequent, near-catatonic lapses of erotic etiquette, a pathology compounded, late in the night, alone with their bewilderment and shame, by intrusive fantasies involving the emulation of subversive acts falsely attributed (as they very well knew) to certain singer-songwriters of their youth, those characters: mostly highly talented but pampered twentysomething millionaire drug addicts assured of a steady stream of narcotics and minimal contact with shared objective reality, the perfect PR versions of their lives sifting down to them through the adolescent white upper-middle class like an unheard-of virus structured so as to remain asymptomatic for decades to come while providing a template for a way of life they could never possibly experience, one that would forever stand in cruelly vivid contast to what actually awaited them when they woke up every day of their future lives, but in the meantime, providing a soundtrack for experimentation with ever-changing, ever-renewed offerings from the burgeoning psychopharmacology industry. One must never underestimate the demand for or the sacramental aspect of legal mood-altering substances, a demand created by those who have never experienced happiness in any other form, and never underestimate their numbers. Now, back to powerful long-acting and highly addictive amphetamines for any and all grade school children betraying, according to the manual composed by psychiatrists pleasantly beholden, specific deviations from proper classroom decorum, meds also serving to acquaint the young with the basics of enlightened retailing and the forming of lasting relationships. I didn't really need a new compass, by the way, I had a spare stashed away all along. I'd hidden it so successfully that I myself have not yet been able to locate it, nothing to worry about, just one of those minor dilemmas that may well be related, though I'm not quite sure how, to a cheerfully gullible and trusting facet of my nature that has always kept my companions in stitches. But the moral of this story has been postponed too long already. It dawned on me only after long years, decades of semesters, the shockingly simple and elegant ratio that states the degree to which I wish to do something is directly proportionate to the necessity of my never, under any circumstances, doing it. I totally dedicated my life to serving and spreading word of this visionary ideal about half an hour ago, and I really feel good. I do, I really feel good.

THE LAST PERSON IN PURGATORY

It seems to be getting a little darker each day. No doubt there are now too few people on earth who believe in its existence to provide the power required to keep the place running; as a matter of fact, the lighting, dim to begin with, has gotten so bad that one is hard put to locate, say, one of those prehistoric telephones that are actually attached to a particular and unvarying spot (they're also all dead) or to make out the wording of signs or directories. Granted, the latter were deliberately designed to confuse and disorient and, without fail, guide you to a sector far from the one you were seeking. Nevertheless, not being able to read them at all is more disturbing than anyone could imagine. I have no idea how long I have been here in this place that resembles a hospital, to the best of my recollection, only one that appears to be infinite; and where I continue to have the sensation of being followed; and where I feel I am constantly bracing myself, even now, for a faraway scream, though I haven't heard or seen a soul in years, and gradually it's dawned on me that I may really be the last person here, can you believe it? Who knows, this may simply be the hush before the cataclysm; perhaps the planet's long-anticipated suicide is nearing—an event guaranteed to produce the most massive and chaotic influx of freshmen ever. Company! But nothing happens, of course, that was all over with long ago, there remains no one but me, me with my tiny bat wings that don't work, like a grotesquely diminutive penis. With my loneliness of such relentlessness and immensity, I can't even feel it anymore; and with this daily renewed hope so hard to distinguish from despair, it has ceased for aeons to be experienced as any emotion whatsoever; a vestigial sadness, perhaps, appropriate to the vestigial body wandering in its coma of insomnia these deserted and interminable hallways, pausing now and then to peer into one of countless operating rooms, the ones with an air of having been vacated moments before I appeared, or spend a minute examining some glittering instrument I've never seen before, its function a mystery: so many tormented into health, so many healed to endure further torment. Then moving on again. What else are you going to do? And wondering, not for the first time, if I have simply been forgotten. I am having great trouble with this. If I have been forgotten, if I have been left here and forgotten.

THE LESSON

Say you finally make it home after a particularly arduous day in eighth grade to find the front door standing open and the furniture gone, and wander awhile through the oddly spacious rooms like a paralytic drowning in the bathtub while the nurse goes to answer the phone. True, you were never the best-behaved little girl who ever lived; still, it seems fair to say that this is the wrong surprise party for you. A little later, looking down from somewhere near the ceiling, you observe yourself letting a cheap unwashed wine-glass slip from your fingers, bending over to select a large section of it from the kitchen floor, and beginning, with intense focus and precision, to inscribe a fairly serious gash in your left wrist. That doesn't work out so well. Locating a dish towel, though, does keep you occupied, then cleaning up the mess you've made. And you refuse to cry. Smart move, you hear a voice say quite distinctly. You might need those tears someday. And you have been telling yourself the same thing all your life.

LITANY

While we slept, we are made of the same things as stars, sang our cells. While we slept, a young priest saying Mass in front of nobody. While we slept, some celebrities broke in and ransacked our home. At one point we got up and shook hands with them, got their autographs, and went back to bed. While we slept, we calculated the amount of money we would want to contribute to the affluent this year. There was still so much good in us, a few sparks of it not yet gone out, at least. We stopped the car a couple of times to let a turtle cross; why didn't we get out of those cars then and there and walk away from them forever? From Pythagoras to Teller is not far, while we slept. While we slept, they could do it, therefore they did it. While we slept, circa 1890, to keep more accurate track of time, they invented a fictitious sun that moves uniformly along an imaginary celestial equator, maintaining a constant rate of theoretical motion equal to that of the actual sun's. What monster dreams up this sort of thing? While we slept, I'm having trouble mastering the new gender-inoffensive grammar. I'm finding it extremely difficult to behave politely and diplomatically at all times. It is not a good sign that we have received visitors neither from the future nor from distant galaxies, according to an illustrious being all brain with mechanical voice—the guy's supposed to be some sort of genius, can't he do something about the sound of that thing? I am rather sorry when I look back, it says, that I ever got involved in this business, a profoundly eschatalogical undertaking if I ever saw one. Don't look at me—I didn't invent that bomb! If I had it to do all over again, I think I would choose a career in the sex industry. While we slept, I'll bet you anything robotboy kept our rare visitor all to himself like a baby mouse in a locked drawer with some bread crumbs and a saucer of water, performing some gory but edifying anatomy lessons, your basic introductory snuff film, obtainable by mail and packaged with immaculate anonymity. While we slept, the world became mainly one endless slaughterhouse of pitiless blind butchers stumbling around, trying not to slip on entrails and gray matter, having it out with the meek, a real mess, and swilling from bottles of excellent Scotch, generally yukking it up all night long while we slept. I have to leave right now to teach a class at the town morgue, where the students at least give the appearance of listening, eyes closed in rapture. While we were sleeping, first we voted into office the ones who watch you drown while very articulately expressing concern; then we tried voting for the ones who kind of like to see you drown. While we slept, no one held a gun to my head. While we slept, I hate my only friend.

MRS. ALONE

Mrs. Alone is always at home. But don't try to phone Mrs. Alone, Mrs. Alone isn't answering anymore. He is writing his poem, leave him alone, will you. The words could still come, startling him awake like the dream of the telephone ringing. Why, he might even try scribbling them down, and he stands a good chance. If he could only overcome the fear, like a deafening dial tone in his right ear where he lies alone all dressed in night listening, listening.

KIERKEGAARD PROPOSES

The older Kierkegaard has entered his front door and is creakily attempting to lock himself in when it comes over him all at once, one last great wave of gloomy illumination: what if God's greatest blessing is to render a person's existence so intolerable, so completely unendurable that the next time he happens to grope for the familiar fear of dying, he discovers it is gone, is nowhere to be found, has in fact been replaced by a simple weightless sense of well-being and peace he had long forgotten he was capable of feeling.

Which shoes should I wear underground? Will a tie be required where we're going? Do I really get to meet them, all the forgotten, the betrayed, the meek sleepwalkers who kept voting for their killers; is it true they will turn for a moment to gaze at me, startled, shyly smiling? Here it is, such a long table, from where we are standing, the endless and poorly lit banquet where the murdered are seated, directly across from their quiet and somewhat neater dates, the executed. And they do, one by one, turn their heads—those with heads—and stare at me a moment, smiling shyly, and strangely rebuke me.

THE NEW JERUSALEM

Nehemiah is pacing the streets at first light, examining the builders' progress and picturing the work that lies ahead. He then gets out of bed, puts on his clothes, and leaves the house to pace the streets, gravely nodding in greeting at the first workmen as they begin to appear; he pauses, suppressing a smile, and contemplates sections of the city's thick walls, the new as well as those that still aren't there. No one can see the great Rose already dawning, looming above them like a spaceship.

PRELIMINARY REMARKS

True concentration is effortless. It is the happy shedding of time, of consciousness itself; the latter appearing to function almost autonomously, the former passing in lucid and controlled euphoria. At this very moment a soundless scream is unfurling inside my head. Late at night as I lie awake in my short narrow bed, the same one I have slept in since childhood, still on my left side fetally facing the wall with legs drawn up sharply at the knees, the always-lighted lamp beside me quivers, imperceptibly, to *you*, perhaps, but not to me, not to me. Uninterrupted concentration, as I was beginning to say, knows no emotions but those that nurture perfect contentment. Have you ever suspected that you were harboring, without your knowledge, the seeds of a destiny you are afraid to contemplate, to name? Just wondering. When it comes to pure concentration, my ideal is to stand perpetually inside the bubble, however fragile, of the present instant, its distant boundary providing a transparent view of the world in all its horror while simultaneously creating a habitat of silence and peace, a hidden numen, a mansion not subject to spacial limitation, rooms countless as numbers themselves. Then I'd be able to hear myself think for once, and all I might have accomplished become a possibility again. Does it seem incredibly dark in here? My name is Raymond—have I said that already?—and the title of my talk today is "Dr. Kafka and the Doll."

NUDE WITH HANDGUN AND ROSARY

The small silver crucified man hangs between her breasts like an arrow directing attention away from the face in its nimbus of unasked-for beauty, all that stands between her and apparition, while pointing the way to the ever inexplicable V, all that's left of her animal: damp, like the tip of a painter's brush just dipped in darkest blue. She has put the thing on like a necklace and gone to admire it in the full-length mirror, in muted light the color of gold's shadow at this late-afternoon hour. There's a light that enters houses with no other house in sight. How describe it? But then there are more important things to think about than light. It lies on the dresser blackly glowing, the one object that's completely self-explanatory here. Just look at you, child with the sun-colored eyes, waiting in line with love's innumerable patients and their grievances at scarecrowlike standstill, how slowly, how badly, they mend; just one more being tested, in need of new double-thick Coke-bottle glasses, straining in the poor light to make out the oversize letters of their own obituaries while they're waiting to be born . . . Soon, soon, between one instant and the next, you will be well.

There is a sound that comes from houses with no other house in sight.

GOODBYE

Each day I woke as it started to get dark and the pain came. Month after month of this—who knows when I got well, the way you do, whether you like it or not. With dawn now, risen from the rampage of sleep, I am walking in the Lincoln woods. A single bird is loudly singing. And I walk here as I always have, as though from tall room to room in a more or less infinite house where the owner's not home but is watching me somehow, observing my behavior, from behind the two-way mirror of appearances, I suppose, and listening, somewhat critically, to what I am thinking. Not too, however. At certain moments I could swear there is even a sense of being liked, as sunlight changes swiftly, leaving, leaving and arriving again. A bird is chirping bitterly, as if these words were meant for me, as if their intent was within me, and will not speak. Nothing is left me of you.

MÄRCHEN

One day, after weeks of discussion conducted primarily by way of circumlocutory and oddly defensive notes irritably passed back and forth in total silence, the Prince and the Mrs. decided to go for a stroll in order to admire the newly green million-year-old elms that densely encircled the castle. This was a transparent lie, one that accompanied them darkly, at least part of the way, for as was well known, both were blind as stones, excellent penmanship, though. Their ulterior if largely subconscious intent was to become hopelessly lost in the forest and apply to several minor writing programs; yet no sooner had they approached escape velocity than they found the way barred by their huge and illiterate shepherd baring his fangs and uttering a continuous low and murderous growl, a constant source of humiliation to the whole family, he's actually quite friendly. At a brisk trot, each clinging to one of his ears, he conducted them home, where they were sent right to bed without supper, execution having been deemed inexpedient.

FIVE AFTER MIDNIGHT

You wake up in an upstairs bedroom of a strange house with no idea where it is. No other house in sight. Although it is completely dark and impenetrably snowing swiftly sideways past the window, somehow you know this. Faraway traffic sounds of New York City at dusk, the dim golden horns of Christ the conqueror approaching, still and sad. You are fifteen, riding the night train south through Germany, and you are having trouble telling half the time if you are awake or asleep, abandoned platforms lit by a flickering greenish fluorescence, signs announcing the familiar names of towns you've stopped at for oddly long periods of time replaced somehow by names unknown: *Klooga, Chelmno, Transnistria, Gurs;* and the ones who are speechlessly staring at you through wire fence, the sun shining right through them—all have the faces of people you know! You grope for the cell phone, but it is 1968 and such devices have not yet been offered for sale to the general public. Damn right too, these things are killing us, but without them how would we ever call home? Good news, ghosts of snow drifting over the highway: soon we shall be a part of all that we now merely see, like that ancient apple tree in Normandy in full blossom, white wind-loosed petals blowing across your lawn, bee-haunted, the sunlit sea, dead leaves scurrying in the wind down West Lorain Street, they look just like countless brown tarantulas. And you are four years old, lying awake to the sound of Seattle's perpetual rain, fog obscuring the rose-colored dawn of Rainier, your snowman sinking back into the ground, hand in giant hand with your father towering above you as he quietly hums Die Forelle, Op. 33; or sings aloud

Ich habe mir ein Kamerad,
Ein besser findst du nicht—

a song of soldiers in the German army, you believe. They must have sometimes sung a few bars, noses black with frostbite; over-all, however, the world was probably not doing all that much singing. Being somewhat closer to their level, you are taking care not to step on the earthworms you've counted as they attempt to cross the sidewalk, it's their job, what can they do. A naked girl of sixteen stands in your doorway reading a letter and smiling into herself. And it occurs to you with unusual clarity that dying is one thing in your life you ought to get right. You must learn to be okay with being alone, but it is also good to know how to befriend pretty much anybody, and fast. As you suspected, no one you terribly miss is in the same state as you, even. Strangely, this has not prevented a lot of them from making an appearance, examining the stupid paintings, or gazing out that window. You are so glad to see them, you would like to cry, but why? What difference does it make? Clearly, they can't hear you, and they never look at you. And you need to get used to that, as these are the final moments of your life.

First light of the long-dreaded day found the loneliest boy in the world fretting intensely and rapidly pacing, counterclockwise, the perimeter of his large room. There. In precisely four hours the door-bell would sound, announcing the arrival, for their long-scheduled playdate, of the second loneliest boy in the world, certainly no laughing matter. Was he up to it? And how would it end? How, for that matter, was it supposed to begin? Well, he'd been there before, and it was time to act like it. There would be the creepy next-to-weightless handshake, that was inevitable; there would be a brief, excruciating instant of eye contact, probably a small "Hi," spoken under their breath, as though to themselves, as they stared at their shoes, a "You know the rules," in so many words, on the parts of their mothers, now come out fighting. He had been the reigning loneliest boy in the world for as long as he could remember. Would this be the fateful day? He quickened his pace, dancing a little, and attempting a halfhearted jab or two at the imagined foe in the vacant air before him. He knew perfectly well that this was ridiculous. There would be no spectators, there never had been, no one to referee, even. In reality, after smiles of maternal encouragement, maybe a suggestion regarding the manner in which they might begin, the two would be left completely alone, and then what? There was always a board game, he supposed, a form of combat requiring minimal verbal exchange. He remembered the time one boy had lowered his guard and offered to let him see his near-priceless No. 1 *Spider-Man* published by Marvel Comics in the early nineteen-sixties in return for the chance to leaf through his own absurdly rare and fragile first edition of the *Pensées*. It was difficult now to believe that he had ever agreed to such a thing. But he vividly recalled the way his opponent, who had himself initiated the lengthy contest involving subtle and remarkably strenuous shifts in posture meant to indicate who was most downcast and bored, had surrendered momentarily and, in a gesture of truce, mutely unharnessed himself from his backpack, deftly removed the slender magazine, and held it out to him. How the two boys had then pallidly drifted apart, all the while, to be sure, keeping one eye on the other, and seating themselves cross-legged in opposite corners, immersed themselves in their reading, successfully killing at least half of the time allotted for their get-together. Then there'd been the boy who simply stood there in the middle of the room, refusing to move, arms hanging limp at his sides and staring straight up at the ceiling for fully fifteen minutes before lowering his chin and drifting slowly across the room toward a window that provided a view of the Hudson goldly shimmering in the morning light far below. He could still feel himself edging in this strange boy's direction, never once giving the impression of deliberately doing so, until finally the two of them stood side by side, each refusing to acknowledge the other's presence, gazing out at the clouds borne relentlessly eastward toward the sea.

"We loathe these coarse documents and flatly reject your transparent attempts to deceive us with peace offers," the captive mouse declared, squinting into the terrible lights, tiny voice quavering slightly, then calm, filled with a splendid indifference, having shed somehow, if only momentarily, the pusillanimity as inexorably linked to its normal existence as gravity, its shadow, its dead children. "We deplore, what is more, shake the dust from our feet and, with all due respect, piss on your condescending attitude toward us, brief smirks of affectionate mockery like the ones children must endure from their elders, your high exchange of amused eye contact, your deniable and unanimous contempt. You are evil that no longer even bothers to disguise itself, enjoying excellent health and psychological well-being. You know perfectly well what you're doing. Deprived of opportunities to dream, even the hardiest, the most heroic of us die within a matter of months. We are only mice, bound to darkness and destitution; we are broken, but we have our furtive pride. In spite of all the harm you do, many of us still enjoy a good quality of life and, God willing, shall continue to for weeks to come. We may be nothing but mice, in perpetual hiding, gnawing at our claws with anxiety. But look at me. Look at me and understand me. We have no interest in your pitiable mansions, no dread of your death-bringing powers. Nothing you do can alter your fate. It is I who shall inherit your complete and merciless eradication."

First there's an infant, and next thing you know there's a ninety-year-old man in the bed, the resemblance is striking! Nobody in his family comments on it, but they are dead, after all. The eyes open, the pale hairless head turns on the pillow as though his father has entered the room. He blinks, like a newborn ostrich; parts and closes his lips as in speech, as under obligation still to explain or otherwise reason on behalf of the person whose date of birth, Social Security number, and name are printed on the plastic band that dangles from his frail wrist. He desists, so sadly diminished the number of consecutive intelligible sounds he is capable of making, what's the use. He is still free, though, to speak to himself, is he not, in his mind, without sound, ah, the joys of longevity. Somebody spoke the first word in the world, he observes; it goes without saying that someone will utter the last. So what was it all about? Considered in this unwithstandable light, what had been the point of putting up with all that shit, and how could he ever have consented to it? Stay in the present, he counsels, though everything points to his having outlived the so-called present, survived to tell the tale, and witnessed its pathetic denouement, and how strange that is, if you ask him. Light is the shadow of God, he'd once read somewhere, a theory now being eerily illustrated by the sunshine coming in through the blinds. I think I am going to leave that to the learned mystics, if it's all the same to you, he groans; for I am surely in no shape to judge, being at present somewhat disoriented, in fact high as a rat (local colloquialism). At this point, having nothing better to do, he takes a close look at his hand. If that is my hand, he remarks, I am going to be extremely resentful. At least it's still there. It is, is it not, about time for my shot, teller and listener in one? He does not put it quite that way, but that's the gist. And can somebody tell me what kind of hospital employs sixteen-year-old doctors? Something is about to happen. And while he is groping around for the call button, all at once it happens.

ROBERT, CAT

He has been my sole companion, sometimes, for days and weeks on end. Prisoner No. 1 and Prisoner No. 2, making do. Yet this solitude cannot compare with his. At any time I can walk out the door—I am not about to do any such thing; theoretically, however, it is within my power. All at once I am ashamed to think that if anyone is anybody's sole companion, I am his. And how many times, absorbed in work or trying to kick its door in, deranged with elation or disappointment, have I turned on him, responding to one of his humorous offers to play by shouting so loudly and viciously that his ears folded back and his sensitive eyes winced as if in the face of heavy winds; and flooded with that male exaltation that comes with any brief distraction from its scared and bitter impotence, how many times have I driven him from my room and slammed the door behind him? How many times, later on, looking for him from self-seeking remorse, have I found him asleep on my side of the bed, or meditating in a circle of sunlight, turning toward me his clear gaze devoid of resentment or hurt or any slightest interest in causing it; found myself in something like the presence of unqualified forgiveness? I will never understand anything except gradually; so gradually that I never really get there. But I know this: his end, when it comes, will be gentle and painless. It will arrive at "the terrible speed of mercy," we'll see to that. And when mine comes, I will know better than to expect from other human beings the mercy that would automatically be shown any sick and incurably suffering stray animal.

LETTER

Thank you for writing to me. It was very kind of you, brought on this trance. I lived again the day we met, the time of day, the light, the weather, season, moon, and wind, I felt it all, from dawn to dark, from gale to the breath of the mouse; I saw it all, except for you. I knocked again and no one came. I broke the lock in vain. At that time I still paid occasional visits to the people who live above-ground, I felt so sorry for them! I pleaded, I implored, I wept; I bared my breasts and raked my nails across them till they bled. But what are you going to do? It's a free country, or it was last time I gave a shit. I know you will agree it is an awful thing to contemplate, but finally you simply have to let go of them and stand there watching as they ascend like big balloons and gradually disappear from view. What a generation. Fucking dreamers, probably still imagine they're entitled to deduct days when the sun doesn't shine! Let them party themselves to death, the ones who're left. Why not? I myself would be willing to pitch in my old circus tents, my collection of antique ten-man hookahs, if we could get a matching government grant, maybe some of that medical-grade pot, and they must have hidden away somewhere a stockpile of all that nonaddictive cocaine they confiscated in the seventies. Little tiny silver spoons for all—also use them to measure out the magical mystery punch, close your eyes and open wide, that's what I always used to say. You'd want to set up an emergency medical station, keep a vat of haloperidol on hand. Maybe throw in a few Nembutal piñatas for old times' sake. Where was I? Oh yes, I was speaking of first running into you—I guess actually we bumped into each other walking backward, our eyes fixed on the sky, goodbye, goodbye, blue balloons. Just two people mistakenly allowed to volunteer for the same hopeless mission. How am I? I'm glad you asked me that. I'm snowing, I'm afraid, I am ghosting over. "Don't come near me," I blizzard. A pose, a sad affectation, it's ridiculous, but it seems to do the trick. To tell you the truth, I don't know how I am. I'm faster, though, much faster, desolate wind in tall pines, a far wind dimly raving, still tearing my hair out; and as I said, I'm eastward, clouding swiftly over, I'm ripped, here and there flashing the new moon's small tit, may the mercies assist me. May blackout strike me on the skull with its big weightless hammer soon. Look. I am flying, flying in my frayed too-small nightgown. I'm bouncing up and down on my bed, fast asleep and loudly whispering something I can't quite make out—my work, that's it, my work. For sleep is my frenzy, my rampage, my furies, while work is my rest, my vacation. I'm running, I am running through high leaf-shorn branches, a wisp of greyhound-colored smoke, and slowing, slowing down now, drifting sideways immeasurably slowly, all those antidepressants, I'll bet. I don't know what I am trying to say, but I am verbal, very verbal: I'm the answer to psychiatry's prayers. I am to the mental health business what a talking pig might be to a veterinarian. One who makes ends meet by moonlighting as a butcher. That's right, I'm the big shiny knife he uses to check his makeup, biographical statement concluded, my bona fide mala fides, don't step in that blogshit, my veil, diagnosis in a nutshell. What I'm trying to get at is this. Our meeting was so brief, I think I exchanged a few shy tongue-tied words with my shoes. I don't really remember your face, I can see it only darkly. What I mainly recall is a kind of white light surrounding and obscuring it, that and talking too much. It's what lonely people do. My eloquence scares me when I'm in the men's room, even if I am always forgetting my lines. But I know what I think when I see it. What I saw was the face of your mind.

GLAMOROUS CAREER

The fact that you happen to be a distinguished and much discussed author proves to be less than impressive to the police departments of most major American cities. This is especially true when you are clearly a horribly dressed twenty-five-year-old drunk who hasn't showered in weeks and is missing a couple front teeth, but what do they know? You *might* be one. Many busy and successful men occasionally neglect their appearance. How about a slice and one Coke per day, a bench in Grand Central Station, and an empty suitcase for verisimilitude's sake, will you settle for that? Where do I sign! And I would like to take this opportunity to register my outrage and disgust at the experimental energy-saving strategy recently adopted in the capital. I realize times are hard, but lighting the streets at night by setting fire to innumerable crucified human beings just strikes me as the wrong road to be heading down. "Look," cries a little boy pointing skyward, "our nation's flag!" More and more it resembles the dress removed from the body of a young woman suddenly struck by at least fifty rounds, allegedly from the barrel of an automatic weapon accidentally aimed and fired at her by an unnamed member of an anonymous branch of our more shadowy mercenary forces as she was wandering through an outdoor market to buy fruit in the early morning sunlight, she and her small daughter arriving in heaven, carried there by gigantic butterflies with the markings of dollar bills on their wings, before their bodies can hit the ground. Which reminds me. Today I would like you to write a brief essay in response to the following question: Who is alive, George W. Bush or Hart Crane? What about this one: work is prayer, true or false? Or: which would you prefer, a seat in the back of the black limousine or an obscure place at the table (down toward the vanishing point) where the serious sit throughout the ages, trapdoors beneath their chairs, each alone in a small circle of green lamplight, with ropes around their necks, keeping it all going? Yes, you have your hand raised? What do I mean by "it"? Well, we've got a beautiful spring day, don't we. Why don't we hold class outside. The boys can don blindfolds and go at each other with baseball bats, or grope around for trees to piss on, while you girls take turns sitting on my lap—let old Uncle Franz tell you all about being a hippie.

What most torments the damned?

The memory of being happy.

And what do they want from us, we who have found ourselves briefly in their midst? What is it they most urgently ask of us?

Remember me. That's all.

Remember me.

It took a couple of hours, but I finally located the building, which was about four blocks away from Mass General's famed psychiatric department where one low-level sadist had gladly supplied me with simple and ingeniously misleading directions. It was halfway between the main hospital campus and Government Center: a large windowless structure without an address, in color a drab shade of shit brown and nearly invisible in its sheer lack of any recognizable utility. And don't ask me how, but after exploring for some time its blank and remarkably Escherlike hallways and stairs, I came upon a door and rang the bell, if for no other reason than that it actually had a doorbell to ring. Then I stood and waited for a thousand years. I was beginning to be sorry I had come, I was starting to be sorry I had ever been born, when somebody opened the door and I found out what it really means to be sorry, extremely sorry. The stench alone, some sort of fecal primate abattoir, almost dropped me to my knees. But it was nothing compared to the sound. Have you ever been close enough to hear the sounds made by a pig when its throat is being cut? Those panicked screams of outraged, hopeless agony and horror might be compared with the choir at the conclusion of Mahler's *Resurrection* compared to what was coming, though eerily miniaturized, from far off beyond that door. It was so terrible I couldn't speak. I moved my mouth a little in an attempt to pronounce your name. It took a couple tries, but at last it was somehow communicated to this man in dirty white who had, to his credit, taken the trouble to answer. He shook his head. It turned out you'd been there only a short time, there is a mercy in the world, however small, and they had sent you home in your permanent sweatpants, pink sneakers, and orange sweatshirt that read BECAUSE I'M THE MOM, THAT'S WHY. Mother of many—what were you, about eleven, when you had your first child—and part-time freelance prostitute. Sitting up talking, late, in the dark cafeteria of the old unlocked, humane, and oddly homey Bullfinch ward, you once kindly offered to blow me for nothing, poor child, how we laughed, and how I loved you at that moment. To me you will always be that frazzled and once-pretty middle-aged twenty-four-year-old; how much I miss you at this moment, the room getting brighter with pain . . . Once I spent an hour or so parked across from your old apartment, looking for drugs, probably, on one of Chelsea's almost comically sinister streets, staring up at your unlit window. Once I approached the door and knocked, knowing no one would answer. Then twenty years went by. I'll never find your number. And I know you will never call me, you idiot. I know I turned away from you—doesn't everyone do that? I want to make it up to you, I do. I don't even know if you're alive. But one of these days it will come to me, I know it, and I will remember your name.

DEAD SEAGULL

Seagull in the corn, postage stamp–size cornfield in the woods, in the middle of the state, and how you ever got here. Weather of heaven, July Massachusetts, the blue sky one endless goodbye. Give me a minute, maggot-swarming preview of the future, give me a moment. You can hone a blade until there is no blade, or dwell with magnifying glass so long on a word that finally it darkens, is not, and fire in widening circles consumes the world. For a moment only, stay with me, mystery. Before you change completely into something other, slow cloud, entrance, spell, not yet remembered name, stay; tell me what you mean. A dead bird is not a dead bird I was once told by someone who knows.

THE REUNION

Incredibly my entire family is gathered and together again in one place. That place, as it happens, resembles a small apartment for one and a half tenants on the Lower East Side of 1979 Manhattan; and I fear there is a severely limited number of spots for them to stand or sit down. Not that anyone seems to mind much. They are standing together in a small group right in the middle of the room, each having assumed his or her expression of choice when just about to have their picture taken. My mother and father both appear to be around thirty years old, and my younger brother has become a grown man somewhat older than I am, with a face unabashedly, even somewhat proudly, ravaged, the digni- fied image of hard years endured at great cost. All their eyes are fixed on me, they are smiling slightly, in a kindly manner, I think, and maintaining an attitude of reticence, tact, and the pleasantly expectant formality of those who have only just met. Also present, I suddenly notice, are both of my stepparents; and accompanying my stepfather is my half brother, the son he will be having one day with my mother. The kid is already a handsome, relaxed, and self-confident eighteen. There's some kind of math going on here that I am not strong in. My stepmother also looks to be eighteen or nineteen, but unlike my brother, she gives every indication of embittered and near-catatonic humiliation, perhaps on account of her several pitiously conspicuous deformities—one of her shoes, for example, is approximately five times larger than the other; and her left hand, with which she is now engrossed in some sort of solitary penmanship competition, has only three fingers, three webbed fingers. It is only fair, however, that in spite of undeni- able homeliness, she receive credit for the nimbus of goodness that auras and follows her every movement, as well as her striking ability to glance across the room at you as though you were, to her, the very dearest person in the world. Unfortunately it's pretty clear that any attempt to compliment her or even allude to these qualities would be met with a sneer of derision, and quite possibly a lightning-swift bite of considerable severity. She's standing alone in a corner of the room at this point, with her back to us, addressing herself in a viciously critical whisper, while gesturing airily with her free hand (a hand perfectly normal in every respect, by the way), her eyes lightly closed, perhaps conducting the opening of a slow and lugubrious symphony she alone hears. A mole comes to mind—a very angry mother mole in spacious gown and bonnet, knitting and rocking with remarkable vigor, some might even say reckless abandon. Actually the mole is deep under the ground at the moment, methodically inspecting even its most remote and peripheral cells, and yet grimly hopeful of making its way to the surface before it gets light out.

CIRCLE

Say I had no choice, this weightless finger touched my tongue and told me to, it taught me; when kinder and more subtle methods failed, it put a gun to my head, a zero seared coldly in one temple, electrode glued chill to the other, the sniffer dogs rooting and snuffling in my crotch, the small white doorless room, the laser flashlight in one eye. You can't hear the voice when it utters let there be speech, yet I faithfully spoke what I thought I was supposed to, inspired idiot, or dummy in the lap of language, the words themselves more real than I, words here before we were and when we are not again. So I blurted it out, my initial soliloquies, what I could catch through the static, giving my head a good thump now and then like one of those black-and-white TV sets, and projecting, those were some vast stadiums, the first row of faces as far as near stars if there at all, never having the faintest idea what it meant, the microphone dead, I did my best, tell them. Inch-thick rope for ascot, eyes put out, chained to my oars, all the others long vanished: the first minute of death is so long, like the first minute of consciousness there in the infinite darkness of somebody weeping, you never arrive, never reach shore, never mind with what clarity you seem to hear with your lips distant roar of surf breaking. I pulled too for those who'd come later, I'm guessing, singing in their names as well, singing twice as loud, strapped to the mast, earways cleared, though I heard nothing but nothing, blue. Making up what I couldn't make out, and all that uproarious and pitiless derision I had to raise my voice above, I mere link—out on that unknown ocean beating at my ears, just as, at the beginning, the mother's heart booming softly; from nowhere it came, like me, months before I arrived to take up the sorry job of being me, whatever a month was, whatever I was then, blind little dolphin with a thumb in its mouth, whatever a mouth was; poor mother mourning her own mother's dying, over the actual ocean she lay, a strong stone's throw from the Ohio or that poisoned ghost of it. Mother of my mother dying away from this world just as I was about to die into it. I see them there, up to their knees, gathered as for a baptism, cross traced in hydrochloric acid on a tiny fore-head, right there at the dead water's edge a scythe of moon, a meteor in arc of falling ax of gold for the severing of hairy umbili-cal rope, hear me out! I saw they were standing watch over her, and my mother's conspicuous absence, wincing at the constant cough; and I saw her whom I would never meet, nearing peace in the scarlet Magdelenean cerements, clenching lightly between thumb and skeletal forefinger the scarlet egg, and the wide river's sundering undertow sucking to its breast her shrunken body, fetal in her narrow bed, nothing but a huckleberry craft by now just vanishing around the first bend, more and more lost from sight by my mother, twenty-two, unaided by lunatic male she'd been sentenced to, from Goethe-phase to Trakl-phase. And she breaks down in her hotel room, in bullet-pocked Vienna, helplessly swept down the blind unwept current still flowing, sadness's chemistry, horror's and guilt's, to this day through my veins, with the unfath-omable fate that sentenced my mother and father to marriage, then me. Months before we met, I listened to her crying, it went on forever, how not hear it, how not be fed it, in a shoreless darkness of sorrowing I listened, still listen, now watch this and pay close attention: nothing else there, only a listening called me, no name, even, till they grave it in stone. Until we finally met, I watched her face rise on the horizon. Her mother was born three days before I was. Then there was some loud mutual screaming in the even more terrible blindness called light. Long before I invented the first word it taught me, it told me the others, so many. So only what was never mine is mine; and when no one is listening, I sing what it means to me, even now, hearing my voice through my own disappearing, farther away every day, my mother's mother's fate and mine now one as I board the ocean liner at three months of age and arrive in New York, filled with space and time.

SONG

Wisteria rain, where is your child-mother? This must be the last bee on earth. So, you find no more grandeur or mystery here? Perhaps you neglected to bring any. Heckling sparrows, vast electron cloud of gnats on windless water. Night blue volume in a language no one reads . . . Are we tired yet? Are you finished debating the blind who insist that light doesn't exist, and have proof of it? Nobody's alone, God is alone. If you liked being born, you'll love dying.

OUR CONVERSATION

Pure gaze, you are lightning beyond the last trees
and you are the last trees'
past, branching
green lightning
of terminal brain branches
numened densely with summer's
hunter color, as night comes,
the ocean they conceal
gone berserk, wind still rising.
Pure seeing, dual vortex doors
to the blue fire where
sex is burned away, and all
is as it was and I am being offered
in your eyes, as in cupped hands,
the water of to never thirst again.
Again I turn away,
the future comes imperceptibly, all at once
towering around me
on every side, and I am lost.
Pure looking, past pain
(this is promised):
we must have wed on poverty's most hair-raising day
delighting, flashing risk, risk
unfailingly lighting the way,
anything possible
in that dissolving of seam
between minds,

no more golden time—
each step I took
the right step, words
came to me finally and, finding the place
you had set for them,
wrote themselves down.
Till true word's anvil ring, and
solid tap of winged blind cane come,
I wish you
all the aloneness you hunger for.
That big kitchen table where you sit laughing
with friends, I see it happening.
And I wish that I could not be
so much with you
when I'm suddenly not; that
inwardly you might switch
time, to sleep
and winter while you went about
your life, until you woke up
well,
our conversation resumed.
Ceaseless blue lightning, this
love passing through me:
I know somehow it will go on
reaching you, reaching you
instantly
when I'm not in the way;
when it is no longer deflected

by all the dark bents, and all
I tried to overcome but I could not—
so much light pulled off course
as it passed within reach, so much
lost, lost in me,
but no more.

October 2, 1999–October 2, 2010

ACKNOWLEDGMENTS

"Circle," "Home For Christmas," "Imago," "Bees of Eleusis," "Blade," and "Our Conversation" first appeared in *Poetry;* "Yes," "Deep Revision," "Song," "The Window," and "The Lesson" in *The Kenyon Review;* and "Robert, Cat" in *The New Republic.* I would also like to express my gratitude to the editors of other journals in which these pieces have appeared, sometimes in much earlier versions, including *MiPOesis, Cimarron Review, Green Mountain Review, Image, Salmagundi, Tuesday, Drunken Boat,* and *Salamander.*

And I would like to thank Michael Dickman, Albert Corn, Patricia Smith, David Young, Peg Boyers, and John Wronoski, who provided encouragement and advice.

The book could never have been written at all without the help of my wife, Elizabeth. All of these writings are addressed to her in one way or another.

A NOTE ABOUT THE AUTHOR

Franz Wright's most recent works include *Wheeling Motel,*
Earlier Poems, God's Silence, and *Walking to Martha's Vineyard*
(which won the Pulitzer Prize for poetry). He has been the
recipient of two National Endowment for the Arts grants, a
Guggenheim Fellowship, a Whiting Fellowship, and the PEN/
Voelcker Award for Poetry, among other honors. He currently
lives in Waltham, Massachusetts, with his wife, the translator
and writer Elizabeth Oehlkers Wright.

A NOTE ON THE TYPE

This book was set in Monotype Dante, a typeface designed by Giovanni Mardersteig (1892–1977). Conceived as a private type for the Officina Bodoni in Verona, Italy, Dante was originally cut only for hand composition by Charles Malin, the famous Parisian punch cutter, between 1946 and 1952. Its first use was in an edition of Boccaccio's *Trattatello in laude di Dante* that appeared in 1954. The Monotype Corporation's version of Dante followed in 1957. Although modeled on the Aldine type used for Pietro Cardinal Bembo's treatise *De Aetna* in 1495, Dante is a thoroughly modern interpretation of the venerable face.

Composed by North Market Street Graphics,
Lancaster, Pennsylvania
Printed and bound by Thomson-Shore,
Dexter, Michigan
Designed by Virginia Tan